LOW-WAGE WORKERS
in
an
AFFLUENT
SOCIETY

Charles T. Stewart, Jr.

 Nelson-Hall
Chicago

ISBN: 0-88229-101-7

Library of Congress Catalog Card
Number: 73-78912

Copyright © 1974 by Charles T. Stewart, Jr.

Manufactured in the United States of America

CONTENTS

PREFACE

Women, teen-agers, nonwhites—the workers who most often receive low wages—have been increasing as a part of the labor force. The trade and service sectors which, next to farming, have the highest proportion of low-wage workers, have been growing faster than the rest of the economy.

Thus the problem of low-wage, low-skill, low-productivity workers remains, despite the continuing growth in per capita income and output in the most productive economy in the world.

This is not another book about poverty, or even about the working poor, although many of the workers with whom it is concerned are poor. It is rather an assessment of: the competitive economic system that rewards some workers well, some poorly; the reasons for the observed differences in pay; and what may be done about the system.

The study arrives at no final answers about what should be done, other than make the market for labor function better than it does. It simply evaluates the potential of various policies, points out the limits to their contribution, and considers their actual, as well as their intended, consequences. For, any policy involves costs as well as benefits, losers as well as gainers.

What should be done partly involves equity in income distribution. This is a larger and a different issue than the distribution of labor earnings. Wages that are low in absolute terms rise in time. Absolute poverty diminishes. But wages and incomes that are relatively low remain. In this sense, the poor we always have with us.

The solution strategy depends upon our concept of the problem. Wage differentials perform an essential function in the labor market and cannot be reduced too much with impunity. On the other hand, low wages that are symptomatic of low industry productivity or of the inadequate development of individual capabilities can be raised through investment in industry and in human capital.

If there is a central finding, it is the old fallacy of composition. What can be done quite successfully for individual low-wage workers—education, training, job placement—cannot be done for all of them because labor supply policies would have to be complemented by appropriate changes in the demand for labor. Policies effective for a few cannot bear generalization to all low-wage workers. They are a diverse group. For these reasons sound and simple solutions break down. There are many paths toward solution, no single one of which will get us very far.

This study originally was prepared under a contract with the Office of Research and Development, Manpower Administration, United States Department of Labor, under the authority of the Manpower Development and Training Act and under the sponsorship of the National Manpower Policy Task Force. It has benefitted from the criticism of members of the Task Force, and in particular from the suggestions of Myron Joseph, Sar Levitan, and Albert Rees. Not all the views expressed would be shared by them, however; they are my own. I am indebted to Mary Weafer for her patient research assistance and to Glenda Howell for seeing the manuscript through final typing.

Chapter One
PROBLEMS AND
POLICY OBJECTIVES

Concern about low-wage workers is stimulated by two separate factors. The first is the correlation between low wages, low earnings, and individual, and/or family poverty. The second is the correlation with low productivity and the loss of output to the nation. From a policy standpoint, our concern is mainly with the second. For, there are ways of relieving poverty and/or its undesirable consequences which are unrelated to the status and characteristics of low-wage workers. Conversely, much poverty cannot be alleviated by policies directed at low-wage workers, because so many of the statistically poor families (below the "poverty line") have no member in the labor force.

In many cases, low wages are not associated with individual or family deprivation; hence, only policies concerned with raising national output are relevant. The worker may have limited needs or may be a secondary worker in a family with substantial income. In a few cases, low productivity is not associated with low pay, but the loss of potential output is still a concern.

The distinction between pay and productivity is important from a policy standpoint. Some policies raise pay without directly affecting the productivity of the individual whose pay is raised, e.g., federal minimum wages. Such policies need not raise output or reduce poverty. Other policies raise productivity, e.g., training or investment, and indirectly raise pay. Labor earnings of low-wage workers may also be increased without any change in either wage rates or productivity by reducing unemployment and underemployment and by increasing labor force participation. Policies accomplishing such results include labor market information and migration assistance; these two approaches both raise material output and reduce poverty.

The concern is with low-wage or low-productivity workers, not with the level of living or poverty as such. The latter pertain to households, whereas low productivity and pay pertain to individual workers. Income is not limited to earnings, and earnings depend upon employment status and hours of work, not just upon wage rates.

The interface between low wage rates and the problems of poverty is, nevertheless, large. First, wage rates are closely related to earnings, mediated by unemployment rates and by hours of work. Second, earnings are related to family income. Few poor families have more than one wage earner, and their average ratio of dependents to wage earners is high.[1] The probability that secondary workers will work for economic rather than other reasons is associated with low earnings of the primary worker in the family.[2] Furthermore, the probability that a secondary worker (in particular, the wife) will have low pay is positively related to low pay of the primary family wage earner.[3]

A final connection between low wage rates and the problems of poverty, mediated by family income, is the tendency for poverty to be inherited. Most of the poor are children of the poor; conversely, a high proportion of the children of poor parents will themselves be poor. Low income is certainly not the only reason for this tendency, but neither can it be disregarded as irrelevant or unimportant.

The association between low wage rates, low family income, and all the associated ills of poverty could be broken by income maintenance, family allowances, and other policies. But our concern about productivity would not be eliminated. Nor may we ignore that substantial proportion of low-wage workers who, because they are not primary workers, or because they have no dependents and limited needs, suffer no serious economic hardship. If their productivity could be raised, and if the cost of raising it were less than the resulting gain, the society and nation, as well as the individual, would be better off. Productivity- and pay-raising policies, where they yield net social as well as net private benefits, are clearly to be preferred to the income redistribution policies such as income maintenance, which may not increase the national product, and in fact, through work disincentives, may reduce it.

The case for raising the productivity and employment of low-wage workers in order to raise their level of living and that of their dependents is unequivocal. Most such workers have incomes below the poverty line as defined by the Social Security Administration. The case for raising their employment and productivity in order to raise national output is less clear. It might be argued that there are more effective ways of increasing the national output, by: concentrating efforts on raising the productivity of workers who already have attained a modest level; hastening the demise of low-productivity domestic industries, rather than devoting public resources to raising their productivity or raising the barriers to foreign competition. However, the cost-effectiveness of alternative ways of raising national output is beyond the scope of this review. It will be assumed that raising national productivity of low-wage industries and individuals is an accepted objective.

One of the ways of raising the earnings and output of workers, whether low productivity or not, is to increase their labor force participation. Many women, and many teen-agers, have considerable discretion whether or not they are members of the labor force, and whether they work part time or part year, or full time, full year. There are millions who moonlight, or who regularly work in excess of a forty-hour week. More people working, and more hours per worker, will raise national output, although not necessarily the rate of growth in national output. The question of how far policy should go in attempting to change preferences in order to increase labor inputs so that national output may be maximized cannot be answered here. Since leisure is also valued and is essential to the consumption of many of the products of labor, output alone is an inadequate indicant of welfare. Nor is all measured output a net contribution to welfare. Basically, welfare results from the optimal output and rate of growth. We are only concerned with involuntary nonparticipation in the labor force, involuntary unemployment and underemployment, and involuntary low earnings. Even if the concept of individual choice is clear, the application is not. An individual may "choose" to receive low wages because he is unwilling to pay the price of raising them through training, education, and mobility.

The nation has an unequivocal obligation to provide employment opportunities for primary workers. It has as an objective the provision of some minimum adequate level of living. As much as possible, this is to be attained through earned income. This in turn implies some commitment to provide more than employment opportunities, to offer a chance actually to be productive and earn accordingly. Since living levels pertain to families, and earnings to individuals, it is not possible to link the two in any rigid way. The number of wage earners and the number of dependents per family unit both vary widely.

The Employment Act of 1946 does not distin-

guish between a national commitment to provide
employment opportunities to primary and to secondary workers, nor does it mention providing
them with more productive, better paying jobs. For
many people, certainly for most, work is regarded
as an economic necessity. Only for a minority of
secondary workers, however, is employment essential to attain a minimum adequate family level
of living. Whatever priority for primary workers
may seem appropriate on the basis of need, equal
increments in income contribute equally to both
family and national income.

Most policies have, or are intended to have,
lasting consequences. But individuals change in
status as primary or secondary workers or in labor
force participation, as well as in need. Some
policies raise productivity in a context of a free
market for labor. There is no effective way of
earmarking jobs or training or other methods of
increasing employment and earnings to a particular
class of workers. Thus, the main thrust of policy is
the improvement of productivity and earnings in
jobs, irrespective of who may fill them from time to
time, and of individuals, irrespective of future
changes in their dependency and need and labor
force status. But improvement of productivity and
earnings is not the exclusive thrust. Judgments on
the relative importance of the goals of optimal
output and improved distribution and on the
priorities among various groups of low-productivity
workers cannot be avoided.

Chapter Two
DEFINITION AND MEASUREMENT

The definition of low-wage workers is somewhat arbitrary. There is no salient cutoff wage.
From a policy standpoint, however, it makes quite
a difference whether the subject groups comprise 5
percent or 20 percent of the labor force. If small
numbers are trained, upgraded, helped to migrate,
or raised in pay, the direct gain to individuals
involved may be a reasonable measure of benefit
because these policies may be assumed to have
minimal repercussions throughout the economy. If
large numbers are involved, however, repercussions which would tend to reduce the net productivity of policies must be considered. For instance,
in order to make training policies productive, it
might be necessary to take measures to alter the
structure of demand for skills. Large-scale training
programs would affect supplies of some skills in
some places sufficiently to change shortages into
surpluses, altering the wage structure and possibly
the methods of production of employers. The

repercussions of these secondary effects on other
workers must be considered.

To raise the productivity of large numbers of
workers instead of just a few, emphasis must be
placed on business investment and innovation and
other policies altering demand for productive labor
in particular skill categories.

In brief, to improve the lot of small numbers of
low-wage workers by almost any policy, adjustments on the supply side may be sufficient. But in
order to improve the lot of a large number of
workers, adjustments on the demand side as well
are required. In order to limit the scope of a survey
already extensive in coverage, a narrow definition
of low-wage workers is employed; policy emphasis
will be placed, therefore, on supply adjustments,
but will not exclude the demand side and will
assume a high level of aggregate demand.

Throughout this survey it has proved difficult
to maintain the distinction between three very
similar concepts: low wages, low productivity, and
low skill. In practice they overlap extensively, but
not completely. In concept they are quite distinct.
Public concern has different bases: with low skill,
concern derives from the belief in the full development of the potentialities of each individual.
Certainly, most low-skill individuals have untapped potentials for more skilled work. With low
productivity, concern is with the untapped national
potential. Certainly the productivity of many low-
productivity workers could be raised to the net
gain of the gross national product. Finally, concern
with low wages derives from feelings of equity:

that earned incomes be in relation to contribution to output, on one hand, that extremes of poverty loosely associated with low wages be eliminated, on the other. Furthermore, there are differences in method as well as objectives in dealing with these three similar but not identical concepts; low skill is an individual attribute, whereas low productivity and low pay are to a considerable extent attributes of particular industries, firms, and areas. The available data, however, compel the use of low wages as the measure of productivity and skill as well as of income.

There is no problem in defining and identifying a low-productivity worker in an occupation or a low-productivity plant in an industry. In each case there are quantifiable measures of output by which relative productivity can be rated. But what is a low-productivity industry? What is a low-productivity occupation? The answer to these questions requires the comparison of unlike products and functions—of unlike inputs. We make such comparisons all the time, by means of prices. Existing ratios (relative prices) tell us, for instance, that textiles is a relatively low-productivity industry and that motor vehicles is a relatively high-productivity industry; by the same token, tool and die makers represent a high-productivity occupation, and fruit pickers, a low productivity one. Labor in one industry, or in one occupation, is more productive than in the other because its products sell for more.

Low productivity can be equated with low value added and associated with low pay when

there is a market for the final product of labor. In
the absence of such a market, however, low
productivity cannot be inferred from a value added
which is not measured by the market; it must be
associated, therefore, with either low pay or with
the specific educational, training, and other prerequisites for the job, as well as with an analysis of
tasks involved in performing the job. A local
government trash collector is a low-productivity
worker because he is unskilled. He may be paid
well. But in most cases, there is no established
market for his services that can provide a value
added measure of his productivity.

A conservative definition of low-wage workers
might be: those workers earning less than $2.00 an
hour when the $1.60 minimum wage went into
effect, including those who were not covered by
the Fair Labor Standards Act, or to whom a lower
minimum applied. Using another measurement
(instead of $2.00), a very conservative definition of
low-wage workers is those whose straight time
hourly earnings are less than 25 percent above the
FLSA minimum applicable at the time. The $1.60
minimum has been in effect for some time (since
1968 for most workers), during which prices and
wages have risen substantially; therefore, upward
adjustments in line with average wage increases
should be made in the definition.

It is questionable whether selecting a somewhat higher cutoff point would make any difference in terms of description of low-wage workers,
analysis of the correlates of low wages, or prescription. As indicated above, however, a substantially

higher cutoff wage, which would include among low-wage workers a large proportion of total workers, would alter the whole solution strategy.

In practice, it is not possible to isolate all those individuals earning below a specific amount, and only those individuals. Instead, it is necessary to select those categories for which data are available which (a) include most of the low-wage individuals and (b) within which a high proportion of the included individuals are low-wage. These statistical categories include:

1. demographic (e.g., teenagers);
2. occupational (e.g., laborers);
3. industrial (e.g., apparel manufacturing); and
4. regional (e.g., the nonmetropolitan South).

There are three approaches toward estimating the total number of low-wage workers. The first is the identification of low-wage industries and/or, through industry wage structure surveys, identification of the number of low-wage workers by industry. The second is identification of low-wage occupations and/or, through census data on distribution of earnings by occupation, identification of the number of low-wage workers by occupation. The third is the use of Social Security and Census Current Population Report data to establish the number of workers and family heads earning less than a specified amount in a particular year, and Survey of Economic Opportunity data on the number and kind of workers with less than specified average hourly earnings. None of these approaches is entirely satisfactory in arriving at an estimate of the number of low-wage workers. However, the objective is not to count low-wage workers, but to establish the correlates of low wages in order to evaluate policies.

Chapter Three
THE CHARACTERISTICS OF LOW-WAGE WORKERS

The characteristics of low-wage industries and occupations as well as the personal characteristics of low-wage workers afford an understanding of the causes of low wages. Among the personal characteristics correlated with low wages are the following: (1) age, in particular, the high proportion of teen-agers among low-wage workers; (2) sex, in particular, the high concentration of females among low-wage workers; (3) race, or the high proportion of Negroes who are low-wage workers. These are attributes that cannot be altered, although their labor market consequences are modifiable. Other characteristics are directly modifiable: (4) low skill; (5) low educational attainment; (6) attitudes and behavior characteristics of a lower-class subculture, or "culture of poverty"; and (7) status as a secondary family member.

To assert that age, sex, and race are personal characteristics which cannot be altered does not imply that their association with low pay is directly causal. The association of these characteristics with low skill is the primary explanation of their correlation with low pay. Discrimination against Negroes, against females, and to a much lesser extent against very young workers and against workers who are not primary workers or heads of families may be a more fundamental explanation. The distinction between personal characteristics and characteristics of the labor market and of the industry and occupation is a matter of convenience, but it is not a natural and clear-cut one.

The labor market experience of low-wage workers also distinguishes them as a group from other workers. The association between low hourly earnings and low annual earnings is strenghthened by (1) high unemployment rates; (2) the high proportion of low-wage workers employed part time or in temporary jobs; and (3) low labor force participation rates. It may appear that low labor force participation is not a pertinent consideration since anyone not in the labor force is not a worker. However, most people not in the labor force at some point in time, except the very young, have been in the labor force and, except the very old, will be in it again. For most adults not in the labor force, this status is a temporary one. Furthermore, the proportion of those registered statistically as not in the labor force who claim that they would like to work but are unable to work or cannot find a job is sufficiently large for a presumption of intent to participate.[1] This intent, as well as the probability of working, justifies consideration of nonparticipation as a relevant aspect of low-productivity worker labor market behavior. These indicants of low utilization of labor apply to other workers as well and are only pertinent to this study insofar as low-productivity workers are differentially affected.

The economic circumstances of low-wage workers are influenced by nonwage benefits as well as by wages paid for work done. An employee may receive paid vacations and paid sick leave. He also may be eligible for medical benefits in case of illness, unemployment compensation in case of loss of his job, disability payments in case of work-connected illness or injury, and a pension on retirement. These benefits and forms of compensation will be paid, at least in part, by the employer. Low-wage workers less often are eligible for any of these benefits and forms of compensation.[2] When they do receive them, on the average, the amounts are a much smaller proportion of their pay than the amounts received by other workers, with the exception of benefits provided by federal law: unemployment compensation, social security, and disability compensation.

Industry

Most studies of low-wage workers have stressed their concentration by industry. The most comprehensive recent study, by Delehanty and Evans, identifies low-wage industries at the three-digit standard industrial classification (SIC) level of detail.[3] The definition of a low-wage industry was derived from a $3,000 poverty income, implying an hourly wage of $1.50 an hour for a full-time, full-year employee, and the definition included the estimate that about 20 percent of all family incomes were below this level when it was chosen in 1964. Thus, a low-wage industry is defined as one in which 20 percent of the employees received less than $1.50 an hour in 1964. After studying wage rate distributions in manufacturing, and allowing about 10 percent for the difference between straight time hourly earnings and gross hourly earnings in which industry wage data are expressed, Delehanty and Evans arrived at $2.12 an hour in 1963, and $2.20 in 1964, as the boundary of low-wage industries.[4]

Low-wage manufacturing industries were found to be highly concentrated in seven major industry groups, as indicated in table 1. In fact, half the employment in low-wage industries was in

TABLE 1
LOW-WAGE MANUFACTURING INDUSTRIES

SIC	Major group	Percentage of major group employment in low-wage 3-digit industries
22	Textile mill products	100
23	Apparel	100
24	Lumber and wood products	60
25	Furniture and fixtures	72
30	Rubber and miscellaneous plastic products	38
31	Leather and leather products	91
39	Miscellaneous manufacturing industries	49

just two groups: textile mill products and apparel. There was at least one three-digit low-wage industry in food and kindred products, tobacco, electrical machinery, and instruments and related products, but in none of these did employment in the low-wage three-digit industry amount to as much as one-third.

Low-wage industry employment amounted to 25 percent of manufacturing employment in 1963. Nearly all (over 90 percent) paid employment in retail trade was in low-wage three-digit lines of trade. The only exceptions significant in employment were motor vehicle dealers (new and used cars) and lumber and other building materials dealers. Most three-digit industries in selected services were low-wage by Delehanty and Evans' definition in 1958; these low-wage industries accounted for 70 percent of paid employment in selected services in 1963.

The approach of Delehanty and Evans, identification of low-wage industries at the three-digit level of detail, results in a total low-wage industry employment of four million in manufacturing alone in 1963. For retail trade the total employment in low-wage industries was 7,638,000 paid employees and for selected services, 2,284,000. In agriculture, employment was 4,687,000. Adding 92,000 in a single wholesale trade low-wage industry, and 1,217,000 in hospitals, yields a grand total of 19.9 million working in low-wage industries in 1963. Most of these workers did not receive low wages, and some workers in other industries did.

The employment totals above are incomplete.

Not all services that are low-wage but only those
appearing in the Census of Business are included.
The limitation to paid employees excludes millions of self-employed and unpaid family members
in low-wage industries, particularly trade and
service. (This limitation does not apply to farming,
whose entire employment was included in the
totals of low-wage industry employment.) Even
with these limitations, the low-wage industry employment total in 1963 was 29.4 percent of the total
employed civilian labor force.

When this total of 19.9 million is compared
with much smaller (although less comprehensive)
totals for heads of family and unrelated individuals
earning less than specified amounts, it is evident
that the industry criterion is not highly selective of
the universe of low-wage workers. About 3.2
million family heads and unrelated individuals
worked full time in 1963 and earned less than
$3,000.[5] Another 4.3 million worked less than 50
weeks in 1963 and earned less than $3,000, and an
additional 0.8 million worked full year at part-time
jobs. There is no way of determining what proportion of these last 5.1 million family heads and
unrelated individuals received a low wage, as well
as earning less than $3,000. There were also many
secondary family workers working full time, full
year and receiving less than $3,000.

An alternative approach to identifying low-
wage workers is their distribution by industry,
rather than identification of low-wage industries.
This approach, however, has only been initiated.
Perrella allocates the five and a half million men

and women working full year in 1965 and earning less than $2,500, but only among divisions, e.g., agriculture, durable and nondurable manufacturing, retail and wholesale trade, etc.[6]

Sternlieb and Bauman use straight time hourly earnings in April 1970 instead of annual earnings.[7] They also allocate the workers earning $2.00 an hour and less—one-fourth of all nonsupervisory workers in the private nonfarm economy—by industry divisions and calculate the percentage of workers in each division earning less than specified hourly wages. Many of the workers included in these totals did not work the full year, and many did not work full time.

It is possible to refine both approaches to identifying low-wage workers by using industry wage surveys conducted by the Department of Labor. An additional source of detailed information on the wage structure of low-wage industries is the annual report to Congress by the Secretary of Labor required by Section 4(d) of the Fair Labor Standards Act. From time to time the report includes special studies of low-wage industries, including in recent years laundry and cleaning services, nursing homes and related facilities, farms hiring workers, hospitals, educational institutions (nonteaching employees), hotels and motels, motion picture theaters, eating and drinking places, retail trade, wholesale trade, and for 1964, nineteen three-digit manufacturing industries. The various industry wage surveys have the great advantage that they offer data on the distribution of employees by small intervals in hourly earnings.

Their drawback is that their industry coverage is far from complete, they are for different time periods, and most industries surveyed have been surveyed infrequently. The one source that provides information on hourly and weekly earnings by detailed industry on a continuing basis is the Employment and Earnings Statistics series. Unfortunately, its earnings data are limited to average hourly and weekly gross earnings of production or nonsupervisory workers.

Bluestone examined all fifty-three Department of Labor industry wage surveys for 1961–66.[8] He defined a low-wage industry in 1966 as one in which average hourly earnings of nonsupervisory employees were $2.25 or less. For all surveyed industries he determined the percentage of male and of female employees receiving a low wage (for 1966, this was defined as less than $1.60 an hour). A few of these industries correspond to Delehanty and Evans' listing of low-wage manufacturing industries; most manufacturing industries surveyed by the Department of Labor however, are at the four-digit rather than the three-digit level of detail. Since Bluestone's work, a number of other surveys have been published as Bureau of Labor Statistics bulletins. Also, a number of reports on employee earnings and hours for various low-wage industries have been published which give earnings distributions for production workers.

The value of all these bulletins and reports is that they confirm the use of an average hourly rate as a surrogate for industry concentration of low-wage workers. Because of their incomplete coverage and different survey periods, these reports cannot be used to refine the approach used by Perella, namely the allocation of all workers earning below specified rates by detailed industry.

The stability of the group of low-wage manufacturing industries was checked by Delehanty and Evans by comparing the 1963 list of thirty-three three-digit industries with that for 1958. Apart from industries for which data were available only one of the years, agricultural chemicals (SIC 277) graduated from the low-wage category, and two industries, miscellaneous plastic products (SIC 307) and watches, clocks and watchcases (SIC 387), moved into it.[9] All three were on the borderline both years, however.

To compare the 1963 list with more recent years, the cutoff wage of $2.12 for 1963 must be adjusted. Two procedures are possible. One of them would adjust for increases in the cost of living, implying a diminishing percentage of workers included as low-wage. The other would adjust for increase in average hourly earnings, implying a constant share of employment included as low-wage, on the further assumption of no significant change in the wage structure. The cost of living approach yields a wage of $2.60 in 1969. Using increases in average hourly earnings in manufacturing yields $2.77.

When estimated average hourly earnings of production workers in 1969 are matched against these cutoffs, all 1963 low-wage industries remain low-wage by the criterion of average hourly earnings of all manufacturing, except other furniture

and fixtures (SIC 253, 259). The following industries that were not low-wage in 1963 become low-
wage in 1969 by this criterion: structural clay
products (SIC 325) and medical instruments and
supplies (SIC 384).

On the other hand, if the cutoff wage is
adjusted by the cost of living escalator criterion, no
new industry is added to the list of low-wage
industries, and the following low-wage industries
in 1963 are no longer low-wage: other furniture
and fixtures (SIC 253, 259); electronic components
and accessories (SIC 367); pens, pencils, office and
art material (SIC 395); sawmills and planing mills
(SIC 242); and men's and boy's suits and coats
(SIC 231).

Occupation

For comprehensive information on the wage
and salary earnings structure of detailed occupations, it is necessary to refer to the 1960 Census.
The census gives the median income and the
distribution by income-classes by detailed occupations. Furthermore, it provides this same information for workers who worked 50–52 weeks in 1959.
For 1959 alone it is possible to know both the
median earnings of full-time wage and salary
workers in an occupation and the proportion of all
such workers earning less than a specified amount.

Delehanty and Evans define low-wage occupations as those detailed occupations in the
Census of 1960 in which at least 23 percent of the
full-year workers earned less than $3,000 in 1959.[10]
This percentage is selected because it is the

proportion of the population below the poverty line at that time. The total employment in 1959 of all females working 50–52 weeks in occupations classified as low-wage for females was 6.6 million (excluding 43,000 in agriculture). This was nearly two-thirds of all females who worked 50–52 weeks in 1959. For males, the total in low-wage occupations was 3.14 million (exclusive of agriculture), less than one-eighth of all working 50–52 weeks in 1959. Inclusion of farmers, farm managers, laborers, and foremen raises the total of males in low-wage occupations to 5.5 million and their share of the full-time employment to nearly one-fifth.

It is clear that occupation, even at the detailed level described by the Census of Population, is not very selective of low-wage workers because of the substantial dispersion of earnings among full-year workers within detailed occupations. Delehanty and Evans' criterion includes millions who are not low-wage, and excludes considerable numbers who are, even among full-year workers.

Many people in other occupations worked full time and earned less than $3,000. Most in many low-wage occupations, on the other hand, earned more than $3,000. Delehanty and Evans limit their count to those working 50–52 weeks. Many, however, worked less than 50 weeks, or less than full time, and for them it is not possible to determine what proportion earned low wages and salaries, what proportion earned less than $3,000 because they worked a short year or less than full time. Data on distribution of annual earnings by detailed occupation are available only for 1959 and are not as finely calibrated as data on industry wage structure. The smallest income step is $500. Since occupational earning data are on an annual basis, they can be converted into approximate hourly rates only for full-time, full-year workers.

The proportions of persons in the experienced labor force who worked 50–52 weeks in 1959 are shown in Table 2.

TABLE 2
FULL-YEAR WORKERS BY OCCUPATION

Occupation	Male	Female
Professional and technical	77.4	38.0
Farmers and farm managers	79.4	65.0
Managers, officials, and proprietors except farm	87.4	75.2
Clerical and kindred	76.4	64.4
Sales	75.4	45.4
Craftsmen, foremen, and kindred	67.9	60.6
Operatives	62.5	45.1
Service workers except private households	66.1	43.4
Private household workers	47.0	37.7
Farm laborers and foremen	42.2	19.0
Laborers except farm and mine	44.7	41.1
Total	68.8	50.5

SOURCE: *Characteristics of the Population*, "United States Summary," Census of Population, 1970, PC(1)-D1, U.S. Bureau of the Census, Table 224.

Workers with low annual earnings who worked fewer than 50–52 weeks during the year cannot be counted unequivocably as low-wage. However, their higher concentration among low-wage occupations suggests that the wage rates of part-year workers tend to be lower than those of full-year workers. The presumption is that within an occupation the part-year worker will earn less per hour than the full-year worker. Thus, assuming the representation of part-year workers among low-wage earners to be in the same proportion as full-year workers is likely to understate somewhat the number of part-year low-wage earners.

There are several methods of refining the occupational criterion of low wages. The Census of Population gives the distribution of earnings by detailed occupation for persons working full year, and permits an actual counting of such persons earning less than a specified amount. But it is only a useful measure of low wages for full-time, full-year workers. Occupational wage surveys conducted by the Department of Labor are for different periods, often for limited areas, and fall far short of comprehensive coverage of detailed occupations. Last, the allocation of all individuals earning a low wage to their major occupations has been done for the poor.[11] The limitations, apart from the problem of determining whether those not working full-time, full-year received low wages, are that the occupational classifications used are too broad.

The industry criterion at the three-digit level did not prove to be very discriminating. One reason is that even low-wage industries include considerable proportions of workers in skilled occupations or in occupations that are not low-wage. One would have expected the occupational criterion to be more discriminating. Most of the detailed occupations are industry-specific, amounting to an occupation by industry matrix at the two-digit level of industry detail and in some cases at the three-digit level. Detailed occupations should, therefore, serve to refine the industry criterion somewhat. But from the very large number of workers netted by the occupational criterion, it is not clear that it is more discriminating for women, although it appears to be for men. To some extent, it lacks the industry detail at the three-digit level. Some important occupations, especially sales and clerical, lack industry specificity. The dispersion of hourly or weekly wages remains substantial even within detailed occupations.[12] In the latter case, neither industry nor occupation nor the two in combination serve as discriminating criteria for identifying low-wage workers. It is presumed that geographic and demographic criteria may serve to account for some of the intraoccupational wage dispersion which renders industry and occupation criteria such crude indicants.

Delehanty and Evans conclude that industry is the relevant variable for identifying the low-wage population, with occupation relatively unimportant. This conclusion is the result of examining the industry distribution of specific low-wage occupations. Many were confined to a single industry. This, however, follows from their definitions: e.g., "laborers, n.e.c., retail trade," etc. It is questionable whether most of these industry-specific low-wage occupations, laborers in particular, are discrete occupations in a functional sense. Information to be presented later on low-wage labor mobility between industries indicates that subdivision of a given low-skill occupation such as laborer by industry of employment is not very meaningful.

It can be maintained that it is the occupational mix of an industry that accounts for its low-wage status. In fact, low-wage industries as a group reveal a relatively high ratio of production to nonproduction workers, and a high ratio of operatives and/or laborers to craftsmen and of clerical and sales to professional and technical employees.

TABLE 3
OCCUPATIONAL DISTRIBUTION FOR
SELECTED INDUSTRIES
(Percent)

Occupational group	Manufacturing	Furniture, lumber, and wood products	Textiles	Apparel	Food
Professional and technical	10.1	2.5	3.3	1.9	4.5
Managers	5.2	5.8	2.9	3.3	7.4
Clerical	12.5	7.3	8.8	7.8	10.8
Sales	2.7	1.9	1.1	2.1	4.2
Craftsmen	19.6	20.7	14.2	7.9	14.2
Operatives	43.1	43.6	63.3	74.6	47.7
Laborers	4.6	16.6	4.2	1.5	7.8
Service workers	2.3	1.8	2.3	1.1	3.8

SOURCE: Calculated from Census of Population, 1970, *Occupation by Industry,* PC(2)-7C, Table 1.

At the broad occupational classification of laborer, service worker, and operative, industry alone is not a discriminating criterion of low-wage labor; at a detailed industry-specific classification of occupations, on the other hand, it appears that interindustry substitutability is high and that, indeed, occupation becomes subsumed under industry.

The relative importance of industry and occupation as indicants of low-wage employment depends entirely on the industry and occupational detail used. Industry at the one-digit level is a less useful indicator of low wages than broad occupational groups. "Laborers" or "operatives" is a more discriminating classification than "manufacturing" or "trade." But at the three-digit level of industry detail, industry becomes more selective of low-wage workers than broad occupational groups. At a corresponding level of occupational detail, most occupations become rather industry-specific and cease to be independent indicators. It is at this level of industry and occupational detail that Delehanty and Evans conclude that industry is the dominant indicator of low-wage employment.

Region and City Size

The regional factor in low-wage employment is primarily a contrast between the South and the remainder of the nation, although the North Central region occupies an intermediate position. Average hourly earnings and annual earnings are lower in the South than in the non-South for nearly all occupations and industries, for both men and women, white and nonwhite, for all age groups, all levels of education, and for nearly all Standard Metropolitan Statistical Areas (SMSAs). Furthermore, the South has more than its share of low-wage manufacturing industries, of farming, and of the associated low-wage occupations. It has a higher proportion of Negroes, of teen-agers, and of workers with less than a high school education. It is somewhat more rural, and its urban population is less metropolitan, than the non-South. On all counts, therefore, it is a low-earnings, low-income region.

Skill differentials are wider, indicating that the differential between the South and the non-South is greater for unskilled and low-skill occupations than for highly skilled occupations, higher for low-wage than for high-wage industries.

Are low-wage industries heavily concentrated in smaller towns and rural areas? Are such industries, as the dominant elements in the local export base in smaller towns and rural areas, setting local wage patterns? Likewise, are lower-wage industries concentrated in the South, and is this regional concentration partially accountable for their low wage? Or, conversely, are these industries located in the South because wage rates are lower in this region? In recent decades the direction of causation is clear. The South's large rural population provided a large labor surplus as farming employment declined sharply. This surplus low-skill labor supply kept wages lower than elsewhere and allowed substantial expansion of employment without upward pressure on wages. Some of the industries relocating in the South, notably textiles,

TABLE 4
CONCENTRATION OF LOW-WAGE
INDUSTRIES IN THE SOUTH

	Surplus (deficit) employment 1960	Relative gains (losses) 1950-60
Agriculture	+532,841	−255,173
Food products	−84,304	+62,925
Textile mill products	+320,236	+124,402
Apparel	−18,309	+113,280
Lumber, wood products and furniture	+154,913	−31,236
Food and dairy products stores	+857	+38,503
Eating and drinking places	−58,635	+19,399
Other retail trade	+45,317	+163,613
Hotels and other personal services	+54,947	+49,751
Private households	+320,860	+37,812
Total	+1,270,723	+323,276

SOURCE: *Growth Patterns in Employment by County 1940–50 and 1950–60,* vols. 5 and 6, Department of Commerce, Office of Business Economics (Government Printing Office, 1965), table 5.

found lower wages an important attraction. Most industries in the South pay lower wages than the same industries elsewhere.

A distinction should be made between low-wage manufacturing industries and agriculture on one hand, and most low-wage services and retail trade on the other. Trade and most services have geographically limited markets. Interregional differences in their concentration in relation to total employment are attributable mainly to differences in per capita income. Trade and most low-wage services also are not very sensitive to size of city. Nearly all changes in relative employment in services and trade occur vis-à-vis population sizes of less than 100,000.[13] Thus, the influence of region and city size on trade and services is largely one-way and limited to wages, whereas the influence on manufacturing is two-way and includes the location of economic activity.

A rough indication of the concentration of low-wage industries in the South, and of interregional trends in the location of low-wage industry, can be obtained from Department of Commerce data on regional (and state and county) share and shift for thirty-two industry groups (primarily at the two-digit level).

Evidence on the distribution of manufacturing industries (at the four-digit level) by size of city shows that industries most of whose employment was outside metropolitan areas were predominantly low-wage.[14]

In terms of the broad structure of occupations, it appears that small towns (and the South) have more than their share of the lowest-wage industries, but that the differences are too small to account for known differences in earnings (see Table 5). Differences in occupation and industry mix cannot go far in explaining the large earnings differentials found between the South and the non-South.

Fuchs studied average hourly earnings in the South and the non-South.[15] He found a differential of about 25 percent in 1960. About one-third of the differential could be explained in terms of differences in city size, and another third by demo-

TABLE 5
EMPLOYED PERSONS BY OCCUPATION AND AREA, 1968
(Percent)

	Total	Metropolitan areas	Small towns	South
Professional and technical	13.6	15.0	12.2	12.6
Managers, officials	10.2	10.7	10.3	10.5
Clerical	16.8	19.5	13.0	15.2
Sales	6.1	6.7	5.4	5.8
Craftsmen	13.2	13.4	13.9	12.6
Operatives	18.4	17.3	21.9	19.0
Laborers	4.7	4.3	5.7	5.5
Service workers	12.4	12.0	14.1	13.3
Farmers and farm laborers	4.6	0.9	3.5	5.7

SOURCES: Hazel M. Willacy, "Employment Patterns and Place of Residence," *Monthly Labor Review*, October 1969, Table 6; and Paul M. Schwab, "Unemployment by Region and in Largest States," *Monthly Labor Review*, January 1970, Table 5.

graphic characteristics of age, sex, color, and education. The differential was inversely related to skill. It was much higher (60 percent) for Negroes than for whites (18 percent for males and 17 percent for females). The relative differential by city size was greater in the South than in the non-South.

Intraindustry and intraoccupational regional differentials also help to account for the high concentration of low-wage workers in the South. Douty summarized the findings of industry wage surveys conducted by the Bureau of Labor Statistics between 1962 and 1966.[16] Average hourly earnings were lower in the South than in the non-South in twenty-three of twenty-six manufacturing industries and in all eighteen nonmanufacturing industries. The percentage differential was greatest for low-wage retail trade and service industries. In manufacturing, except for one paper and two chemical industries with earnings higher in the South, the percentage differential is smallest for the low-wage cigar and textile industries, all of them heavily concentrated in the South.

Hoffman studied the average earnings for many occupations, including low-wage occupations such as janitor, laborer, and watchman for February 1967.[17] Occupational wages were invariably lower in the South, and by a wide margin, in the low-wage occupations, although not always lower, and never much lower, in skilled occupations. Among industry divisions, earnings were lowest in retail trade in the majority of cases. Blackmore examined average hourly earnings differentials between male janitors and a wide range of other occupations, thirty-nine male and twenty-three female, in 1966–67.[18] The South had the largest differentials for fifty-one occupations in manufacturing, and for forty-seven in nonmanufacturing (of the twenty-six exceptions, twelve were truck-driver occupations). In nearly every case, differentials in the South were greater in nonmanufacturing than in manufacturing.

Hoffman also examined relative earnings in 1966–67 for three occupational groups: office clerical, skilled maintenance, and unskilled plant workers in eighty-three metropolitan areas. The positive relation between city size and earnings was confirmed. Differentials between Southern and other metropolitan areas were only clear-cut for the unskilled workers, whose earnings in the South were much lower for all city sizes, indicating a wider skill differential in the South than in the non-South.

Douty also compares Southern metropolitan areas with all metropolitan areas combined, for the same three occupational groups: office clerical, skilled maintenance, and unskilled plant workers. He confirms Fuchs' findings of a direct relation between city size and earnings and consistently much greater differentials for unskilled workers than for the two skilled groups.

Individual Characteristics

Industry, occupation, and region and city size are useful indicants of the concentration of low-wage workers and help account for their low wages. They do not, however, identify all low-wage workers, nor adequately explain their earnings. Individual characteristics must be examined to predict, if not to explain, wage differences within occupations, as well as between occupations, for a given industry or region.

Age

Although there are two age groups with low earnings, the very young workers and workers 65 and over, attention will be devoted only to young workers on the assumption that most of the policies concerning low-wage workers are not pertinent to those over normal retirement age. Furthermore, except for those working on farms, many of the older workers may not receive low wages; they work less than full time. Of all workers aged 16–21 with earnings in 1971, only 4.1 percent earned more than $3,000; 73 percent earned less than $1,000.[19] (Most of the very low earners worked less than full year or less than full time or both.) In terms of median hourly earnings, 16–17-year-olds received $1.58 in October 1969, whereas 18–19-year-olds received $1.87.[20]

Teen-agers are overrepresented by a factor of three as laborers, both farm and nonfarm. They are overrepresented by a factor of nearly two as service workers. They are slightly overrepresented also in clerical and sales jobs.[21] There is a marked difference in occupational distribution of employed teen-agers who are 16–17 and teen-agers aged 18 and 19.[22] The proportion of teen-agers in professional and technical, operative and clerical occupations rises sharply but in sales declines for both sexes. The occupations of craftsmen and foremen rise sharply, whereas farm and laborer occupations fall markedly for males, and for females service occupations fall. If this shift is simply a function of age, it would be very encouraging, although the occupational distribution of 18- and 19-year-olds is still very different from that of the total work force. If, on the other hand, the improvement in occupational distribution for older teen-agers is simply an attribute of two quite different groups, one entering the labor force at a very young age and the other entering later, then the findings are less encouraging.

Teen-agers are not a homogenous group. The main differentiation appears to be educational attainment. When students 16–17 are compared with students 18–24 years old, the older group shows an occupational distribution far more favorable than the younger group.[23] When students are compared with nonstudents of the same age, they reveal a higher-wage occupational pattern.[24] The most striking finding, however, is the contrast in broad occupational group between high school graduates and high school dropouts.[25]

Table 6 indicates significant differences in broad occupational group for teen-agers as a function of high school completion, particularly for females. More important, it suggests considerable upward occupational mobility as a function of age for males who completed high school but not for dropouts, nor for women in either educational category.

The first problem of teen-age workers is their

TABLE 6
OCCUPATIONAL DISTRIBUTION OF HIGH
SCHOOL GRADUATES AND DROPOUTS, 1968
(Percent)

	Percentage Employed in Occupation			
	White collar	Blue collar	Service	Farm
Male high school graduates, 1968	20.3	65.4	8.9	5.5
Men 25–44 with 12 years of schooling	37.5	52.3	6.3	3.9
Male high school dropouts, 1967–68	14.9	69.0	9.7	6.2
Men 25–44 with less than 12 years schooling	14.5	73.5	6.0	6.1
Female high school graduates, 1968	66.9	16.4	15.7	—
Women 35 and over with 12 years of schooling	69.7	13.3	15.4	—
Female high school dropouts, 1967–68	29.4	29.5	37.9	—
Women 35 and over with less than 12 years of schooling	26.2	31.0	39.8	—

SOURCE: Vera C. Perrella, "Employment of High School Graduates and Dropouts in 1968," *Monthly Labor Review*, June 1969, pp. 38, 40.

high rate of unemployment—more than three times that of all workers; the second problem is their low pay. The seriousness of each of these problems depends upon the status of teen-agers as primary workers, i.e., their need for employment and income.

Studies have revealed that the need for employment and income, as defined by a status as a primary worker and as a head of household, is inversely related to the unemployment of teen-agers. Married teen-agers have a much lower rate of unemployment than unmarried. Much of the high unemployment rate among teen-agers is the result of their casual attachment to the labor force, their limited need for income.

Low earnings, on the other hand, are attributable to lack of experience, lack of skill, low productivity compared with adult workers, higher nonwage costs of employment due to exceptional need for training and for supervision, and high turnover rates.

The optimist views the problems of teen-age workers as not serious, as temporary and self-eliminating by the simple process of aging. The pessimistic view, on the other hand notes that teen-age workers and workers aged 20–24 are not the same people a few years apart in age. Most workers 20–24 years of age were not in the full-time labor force before the age of 18, and many not even at 18 or 19. Demographic trends are on the side of the optimist. Teen-agers throughout the 1960s have been rapidly increasing in number, and have been an increasing proportion of the labor force (the number of teen-agers nearly doubled between 1950 and 1970). Rising teen-ager unemployment rates can be attributed in part to this demographic trend. In the 1970s, however, the number of teen-agers will level off and begin declining; the proportion of the labor force consisting of teen-agers will decline for many years ahead. Thus, future prospects are considerably brighter than the recent past would indicate.

Sex

Females earning less than $2,500 in 1963 totalled 21 percent of the female full-time, full-year workers. The corresponding figure for males was 9 percent.[26] Women are overrepresented in low-wage occupations and industries despite the fact that a higher proportion of women than men complete every level of education through high school. A somewhat higher proportion of female workers than of male workers is nonwhite, because nonwhite labor force participation rates are higher than white participation rates for females, but lower for males. A smaller proportion of female workers, however, consists of very young workers because of low labor force participation rates in the childbearing period. This is a favorable factor, since both occupation and earnings tend to improve with age. Another favorable factor is the higher participation of females in large cities. The lower rates in small cities and rural areas undoubtedly resulted from lack of appropriate jobs.

It was possible to arrive at a rough measure of female representation in low-wage industries as defined by Delehanty and Evans through the Department of Labor's employment and earnings statistics. Females were slightly over half of all employees in low-wage manufacturing industries in 1963, although they were only 26 percent of total manufacturing employment. In retail trade it was not possible to match all of the Census of Business three-digit industries, but the exceptions that occurred were small. Slightly under half of all low-wage retail group employees were females. In selected services most employment is in low-wage groups, and for the major group as a whole, slightly over half of the employment was female. Hospital employment was 80 percent female. Of the major groups, then, only agriculture, almost exclusively male, did not have a heavy overrepresentation of females.

Bluestone's summary of industry wage surveys for 1961–66 further reveals that in all industries male average hourly earnings were higher than female, and the proportion of female workers who were low-wage was higher than the proportion of males in all but one industry (cigars in 1964).[27] Most of the lowest-wage industries had a preponderance of female employees (the same is true of the lowest-wage trade and service industries), but most of the somewhat higher-wage (although still low-wage) industries had a preponderance of male employees.

Evidence of the concentration of women in low-wage occupations has already been presented: nearly two-thirds of females employed full time, full year in 1959 were in low-wage occupations as defined by Delehanty and Evans. Oppenheimer has studied the "sex-labelling" of jobs, finding the concentration of women in occupations with 70 percent or more of the workers female almost as great in 1960 as in 1900.[28] Of her list of thirty-one occupations, accounting for 51.5 percent of the female labor force in 1960, all but two, teachers and office machine operators, fit Delehanty and Evans' definition of low-wage.

The U.S. Equal Employment Opportunity Commission has published data on the employment of women in the twenty industries (two-digit mainly) that are the leading employers of women.[29] The data for 1966 (published annually through 1970, but in less accessible format), corroborate the conclusion based on the 1960 census that the low-wage concentration of women is associated both with their concentration in low-wage industries and their concentration in the low-wage occupations in each industry. In addition, however, the evidence of the 1960 census is that in almost every detailed occupation, the annual earnings of women working 50–52 weeks were substantially lower than those of men.[30]

Race and Ethnic Group

Over 92 percent of all nonwhites in the United States are Negroes. Four other racial groups are distinguished in the Census of Population: Japanese, Chinese, Filipino, and American Indian. Each of these racial groups has its own distinctive industry and occupation distribution pattern (see table 7). Both Japanese and Chinese have distributions which, except for Chinese concentration in services, compare favorably with the white occupational distribution. Japanese exceeded white workers in median incomes in 1970. At the other extreme, American Indians had median incomes significantly lower than those of Negroes and a quite unfavorable occupational distribution. Filipinos and Chinese occupied an intermediate posi-

TABLE 7
OCCUPATIONAL DISTRIBUTION OF EMPLOYED PERSONS BY ETHNIC GROUP 1970
(Percent)

	White	Negro	Japanese	Chinese	Filipino	American Indian	Spanish Surname	Puerto Ricans in United States	Puerto Rico
Professional and technical	15.6	8.3	19.0	25.1	23.6	11.7	6.1	13.4	5.5
Managers, officials, proprietors	9.0	2.3	8.2	8.5	2.4	4.4	4.2	6.2	3.2
Sales	7.7	2.3	6.4	4.7	2.7	3.9	4.3	7.0	4.3
Clerical	18.4	13.7	20.2	18.0	17.2	16.0	13.0	14.7	16.7
Craftsmen and foremen	14.4	9.0	11.8	5.0	8.3	14.6	16.2	12.2	11.5
Operatives	16.9	23.7	11.7	15.2	12.9	21.9	26.2	21.2	35.6
Laborers except farm	3.9	9.4	5.9	2.3	5.2	6.8	9.0	5.3	5.8
Service workers except household	9.7	20.0	11.0	19.6	18.7	16.6	12.8	11.8	15.9
Private household workers	1.3	8.3	1.8	1.0	1.1	2.9	1.6	2.4	0.4
Farmers and farm managers		0.6	2.0	0.2	0.5	0.2	0.4	1.1	0.1
Farm laborers	3.1	2.4	1.8	0.2	7.3	1.3	6.1	4.7	1.0

SOURCES: U.S. Census of Population: 1970, Final Reports PC(1)-C53, PC(2)-1B, 1C, 1D, 1E and 1G, and PC(2)-7C.

tion between the Negroes and the whites in occupation and income.[31]

From the viewpoint of low-wage workers, the second largest ethnic group, half as large as the Negro, comprises persons of Spanish background. This is a diverse group. At the time of the 1970 Census, 94 percent of "persons of Spanish surnames" were classified as white. This group was concentrated in the Mexican border states from Texas to California, plus Colorado. It was predominantly American, with most foreigners being from Mexico. New York (where most people with Spanish surnames were Puerto Ricans) is the center of concentration of Puerto Ricans. Since 1960 the main change in composition has been the influx of over 600,000 Cubans, about half of whom settled in the Miami area. Not all individuals of Spanish surname are of Spanish language or culture. Nor do all members of the Spanish ethnic group have Spanish surnames, but most do.

Whereas Chinese, Japanese, and Filipinos are predominantly in the high-wage West, and nearly half the American Indians are also in the West, Negroes are still heavily concentrated in the South. People of Spanish background, on the other hand, have three distinct centers of concentration: California and the Southwest, New York, and Puerto Rico itself. (Miami might be considered a fourth center, distinguished by the dominance of foreign-born Cubans.)

Industry and occupation by race (Oriental, American Indian, Negro) and by Spanish surname for 1966 is provided by the Equal Employment

Opportunity Commission (EEOC) for 26 million workers, including nearly all the workers in establishments with 50 or more employees, with breakdowns for sixty industries and for nine broad occupational groups. Negroes are overrepresented by a factor of two or more in: agriculture, tobacco manufactures, water transportation, eating and drinking places, hotels and other lodging places, personal services, repair services, and medical and other health services.[32] Spanish-surname individuals are overrepresented by a factor of two or more in: agriculture, apparel manufacturing, miscellaneous manufacturing industries, water transportation, transportation services, eating and drinking places, hotels and other lodging places, and personal services.[33] In brief, both groups are overrepresented in low-wage and underrepresented in high-wage industries. Unpublished data from the EEOC for 1971 reveal progress, but the general conclusion stands. Within each industry, Negro and Spanish-surname males are overrepresented in the lower-pay occupational groups (with one exception: coal mining). Females fare slightly better, with Negro females doing better than non-Spanish white females in retail trade and brokerage, and Spanish-surname faring as well as or slightly better than white females in ten industries.[34]

Since many very small firms are not required to report, the EEOC data are not representative of the entire labor force for farming, trade, and for some services and their related occupations. Table 8 suggests that the occupational distribution of Negroes is worse for the EEOC-reporting firms that for the very small firms omitted from EEOC

TABLE 8
OCCUPATIONAL DISTRIBUTION BY ETHNIC GROUP, 1971
(Percent)

| | EEOC-reporting Firms | | All Employed Workers | |
	Negro	Spanish surname	White	Nonwhite
Professional and technical	5.3	5.7	14.6	9.0
Managers, officials	2.0	3.0	11.8	4.1
Farmers, farm managers	—	—	2.3	0.7
Clerical	12.9	13.5	17.4	13.7
Sales	4.0	5.7	6.9	2.3
Craftsmen	7.3	10.9	13.5	7.9
Operatives	31.7	29.0	15.8	21.7
Service workers	18.5	11.8	11.8	27.6
Laborers	18.4	20.4	4.5	10.3
Farm laborers	—	—	1.6	2.6

SOURCES: Unpublished data from the U.S. Equal Employment Opportunity Commission; *Manpower Report of the President,* 1972, p. 173.

coverage. It is difficult, however, to equate a manager or professional in a large firm with one in a very small firm.

The EEOC also provides breakdowns by state, SMSA, and selected counties for selected industries. These breakdowns allow the study of regional differences in occupational and industrial concentration. They also permit a rough comparison of the several centers of population of Spanish background. Data for Miami, for instance, reveal a pattern slightly more encouraging than that for the country as a whole.[35]

An index of occupational position was calculated by giving each of nine broad occupational groups a weight proportional to its median earnings, in 1959, by sex. The occupational position of the Negro relative to the anglo (white person with non-Spanish surname) was lowest in the South both for males and females (and considerably lower for males than for females). This was not true, however, of the other groups, whose population concentrations lie outside the South.[36]

Negroes fare poorly in earnings, even after allowing for their distribution by occupation, industry, and region. Their earnings in given occupations are less than white earnings.[37] White–nonwhite occupational wage differentials are largest in the South, and in the South they are largest for low-wage occupations in which the overconcentration of Negroes is particularly notable.[38] The high Negro concentration in low-wage occupations in the South partially accounts for greater interoccupational differentials in the South than in the non-South, and also for the fact that South–non-South occupational differentials are greater in low-wage than in higher-wage occupations.

Negroes are heavily concentrated in the younger age groups (this is also true of the population of Spanish background and of American Indians) because of high birthrates in recent decades. This unfavorable age structure is aggravated by lower school enrollment rates for Negro than for white teen-agers. The growth of occupational earnings as a function of age is slower for Negroes than for whites.[39]

The median education of nonwhites in the labor force was 12.0 years in March 1972, compared to 12.5 years for whites. Thirteen years earlier the gap was 3.4 years. This rapid closing of the gap means that older Negroes lag far behind their white contemporaries in formal education, whereas for the age group 25–29 the average educational attainment is almost identical (12.4 years for Negroes and 12.7 for whites in 1972).[40] However, at given levels of education Negroes earn considerably less than whites. This is not entirely the result of lower occupational earnings. For given levels of education, Negroes have a less favorable occupational structure. For instance, 11.4 percent of Negro high school graduates worked as nonfarm laborers in March 1967, contra 3.8 percent of white high school graduates. The corresponding figures for service workers were 17.2 and 6.5 percent.[41]

Negro females have higher labor force participation rates, and Negro males have lower participation rates than their white counterparts at every age except the youngest. This high proportion of females increases the number and share of low-wage workers in the Negro labor force. Unemployment rates for Negro males, typically twice the white rate, prove to be even higher, nearly three times the white rate, when adjusted for Negro male underparticipation in the labor force.[42]

Education

The positive relation between number of years of school completed and income has been the subject of numerous investigations in recent years and has become an accepted part of the American faith. Income is closely related to earnings and wage rates. It is not surprising to find considerable variation in median school years completed among broad occupational groups. For 1967 these groups' distribution by years of school completed is shown in Table 9.

TABLE 9
EDUCATIONAL ATTAINMENT BY
OCCUPATIONAL GROUPS
(Percent)

	Less than High School	High School	More than High School	Median Yrs. 1967	Median Yrs. 1971
Farm laborers and foremen	63.1	19.9	7.0	8.6	10.0
Private household workers	76.0	20.2	3.8	8.9	9.5
Farmers and farm managers	64.2	27.7	8.1	9.1	10.0
Laborers except farm and mine	71.1	23.8	5.1	9.5	11.1
Operatives and kindred	61.0	33.4	5.6	10.8	11.4
Service workers except private house	54.6	35.2	10.2	11.5	11.9
Average, all workers	39.0	36.7	24.2	12.3	12.4

SOURCES: "Educational Attainment of Workers March 1967," Bureau of Labor Statistics, Special Labor Force Report no. 92, p. A-14. Years of school completed by detailed occupation are given in "Occupational Characteristics," Census of Population, 1960, vol. 2, Final Report PC(2)–7A, tables 9–11. Source for 1971 is *Manpower Report of the President*, 1972, p. 207, which gives a combined figure for all farm workers, including farmers.

Occupational differentiation by educational attainment is clear-cut: the great majority of people in low-wage occupations and industries have less than a high school education, and the majority of individuals with less than a high school education are in such industries and occupations.[43] This second statement is less true of older workers, because the high school diploma as a screening device was less important at the time they entered the labor force. The last column in Table 9 indicates, however, that the average educational attainment of low-wage occupations has been rising rapidly in recent years, closing the gap in educational attainment between them and the median for the total labor force.

Information on the education of workers by industry is available from the 1970 census. (The industry breakdown does not correspond in many cases to that used by Delehanty and Evans.) Although low-wage industries typically have employees with below-average educational attainment, the relation is not clear-cut. Some trade and service industries have median years of schooling that are high compared to manufacturing industries with similar average earnings. (These discrepancies seem related to the sex ratio of employment in an industry.)

Duncan has suggested that differences in earnings as a function of education are mainly attributable to the relation between education and occupation.[44] Other studies indicate that within an occupation differences in earnings related to differences in education are small.[45] It may be inferred

TABLE 10
MEDIAN YEARS OF SCHOOL COMPLETED
AND EARNINGS,
EXPERIENCED MALE WORKERS IN
SELECTED INDUSTRIES, 1970

	Median years of school	Median earnings*
Agriculture	10.1	$5,124
Manufacturing	12.2	8,849
Lumber and wood products	9.9	6,465
Furniture and fixtures	10.7	6,719
Textile Products	10.3	6,318
Apparel	11.5	7,613
Food and kindred products	11.8	8,234
Canning and preserving	11.1	8,197
Bakery products	11.7	8,070
Leather products	10.6	6,222†
Retail trade	12.1	7,668
Food stores	11.9	7,642
Eating and drinking places	11.4	6,807
Personal services	11.6	6,564
Private households	9.3	3,868
Hotels and other lodging places	10.9	6,112
Laundering, cleaning, dyeing	11.6	7,143
Barber and beauty shops	11.6	6,438
Hospitals	12.6	7,206
Entertainment and recreation	12.2	7,732
Total experienced male labor force	12.3	8,633

SOURCE: Census of Population: 1970, "Industrial Characteristics," Final Report PC(2)-7B, Tables 3, 11.

*Workers employed 50–52 weeks during the year.
†Shoes only.

that the relation between industry earnings and the educational level of workers in the industry is largely explainable in terms of occupational mix.

Denis Johnston, studying the educational attainment of workers, found that 85 percent of the increase between 1940 and 1960 was within occupations; only 15 percent reflected movement of workers into occupations requiring more formal schooling.[46] Workers with some college education are becoming more widely dispersed among nonprofessional white and blue collar occupations. Between October 1952 and March 1965, the largest relative increases in the proportions of workers with twelve years of education occurred among laborers (13.8 to 23.9 percent) and service occupations (19.7 to 31.8 percent) and were also large for farm occupations and operatives—in sum, for the lower-wage occupational groups. The gains in education have been more striking among nonwhites. During the 1940s, the increase in the number of workers with four years or more of high school education was greater than the increase in need, as measured by Johnston. This suggests that individual job prospects depend more on relative than on absolute educational attainment as levels and expectations rise.

The differences in median income in 1967 between workers with less than eight years of school and with four years of high school, or more, were greatest for service workers ($1,750 for whites, $1,000 for nonwhites) and for craftsmen ($1,300 and $1,400), least for nonfarm laborers ($450 and $1,050) and operatives ($750 and

$1,250). For three of these four occupational groups, the absolute differential by education is greater for nonwhites than for whites.[47] Because of rapid gains in education of nonwhites, median years of school completed is a deceptive indicator without adjustment for age.

The unemployment rate is inversely related with years of school completed (except for workers with less than eight years of school, concentrated in older age groups and in farming). The disparity between employed and unemployed workers in median years completed has shown no systematic change. It is less pronounced among nonwhites than among whites. Labor force participation rates are directly related to educational attainment (except for very young age groups, with many still in school).[48]

So far as low-wage workers are concerned, education is unlike other demographic characteristics. The differences in educational attainment by sex are small; fewer males finish high school, fewer females finish college. Age is a factor in that older workers on the average have completed fewer years of school than younger workers. It is also a factor among very young workers, many of whom have not yet completed their schooling. This factor is not very important in considering low-productivity workers, however, since they are predominantly without a high school degree, and most young workers who have not completed their education go beyond high school. Education is a significant factor, however, differentiating whites and nonwhites, specifically Negroes. It also differentiates Americans of Spanish background. Although differences in median years of school completed are diminishing rapidly, and are small for young adults, the difference in the proportion of whites and nonwhites currently finishing high school is still substantial.

Regionally, the South is well below the Northeast and West, and slightly below the North Central area, in educational attainment. More significantly, average earnings for males at a given level of education are lower in the South for every level of education and almost every occupational group. The differential is greatest for the lowest-wage occupational groups, and greater for nonwhites than for whites.[49]

The advantages of education are smaller for women than for men. For a given level of education, their occupational distribution is toward lower-wage jobs. Although the educational attainment of men and women in an occupation is rarely far apart, invariably the earnings of women are lower. The same conclusions apply to Negroes. Their occupational and industrial distribution for a given level of education is less favorable than that of whites, and for a given occupation their earnings average well below that of whites.[50] Lassiter, who studied the relation between income and education for males only, concluded that the return to incremental schooling was less for nonwhites than whites, but was greater for whites in the South than in the non-South.[51] The inference is that the white–nonwhite differential gain from education is wider in the South than elsewhere.

Finally, as already noted, there is a significant difference in the occupational distribution of teen-age high school graduates and of dropouts. There is a large difference in the occupational distribution of male adult and teen-age high school graduates, but not for adult and teen-age dropouts or for females, suggesting that the high school diploma offers entrée to career ladders and/or is a step toward additional education for males much more than for females.

Secondary Workers

The only reason to distinguish between secondary and primary workers is distributional. The need for employment and for higher wages is presumably less if a worker is not the only or the main source of support for a family. But earnings are not the only source of income, and a family's income adequacy cannot be expressed in terms of the number of wage earners. The very concept of a married woman as a secondary family worker is becoming more dubious. When she has essentially the same attitude toward labor force participation as a man, there is no reason other than obsolescent tradition for listing her as a secondary family worker.

There are no data classifying low-wage workers by secondary family worker status, nor data classifying secondary family workers by industry and occupation. But there is indirect information that a high proportion of women and of teen-agers in the labor force are secondary family workers. In 1967 the gross number of secondary workers, defined as the number of earners per family minus one, was 35.5 million.[52] The total number of individuals is well in excess of employment or of labor force (which averaged 80.8 million for the year, including 53.8 million primary workers). Movements into and out of the labor force are far more important for secondary than for primary workers, thus overstating the ratio of secondary to primary workers when the number of different individuals, rather than the average number at any one time, is counted. The ratio was somewhat higher for Negroes than for whites. The majority of secondary workers—70 percent in 1966 —are married women with husband present.[53] Most of the remainder are teen-agers. In March 1967 the number of teen-age children in the labor force who were living with one or both parents (nearly all of whom were presumably secondary family workers) was 5.9 million, or 17 percent of the gross total of secondary workers for the year.[54] Additional teen-age wives not living with parents were secondary workers. The civilian labor force aged 16–19 for the year as a whole was 6.5 million. Although the sources are not quite comparable, the conclusion is clear: the preponderance of teen-agers are secondary workers. The concentration of secondary workers by occupation (and inferentially, by industry) can be approximated from Census of Population data on the number of earners by subtracting the number of family heads by detailed occupation. Other sources are available for married women. Of 26 million females working in 1966, 14.6 million were wives with husband present and 13.3 million with husband employed— clearly secondary family workers. One would not expect the distribution of over half the female workers to differ much from the total, and it does not.[55] Occupations with a high ratio of total workers to family heads almost invariably have a high proportion of females. Most of these occupations are low-wage.

Disability

One possible contributing factor to low wages, high unemployment, and low labor force participation is poor health and disability. The evidence on disability is clear-cut.[56] Of all persons in the labor force aged 25–44 in 1962, 9.3 percent of those employed and earning $7,000 and over had restricted activity for reasons of health; the rate for the employed earning less than $2,000 was 14.6 percent. The rate for all unemployed workers in this age group was 21.4 percent, compared to 10.5 percent for employed workers. Although the relation between income and rates of chronic conditions is not as clear-cut as that between income and restricted activity rates, the proportion of workers with restricted activity related to chronic conditions was 14.6 percent for the employed earning $7,000 and over, 23.1 percent for those earning less than $2,000, and 34.8 percent for the unemployed.

Disability rates are higher for low-wage occupations; for every occupation, they are higher for the unemployed than for the employed. Occupations with the highest rates of activity limitation among the employed in 1962 were farmers (24.3 percent), private household workers (16.5 percent), farm laborers and foremen (15.3 percent), service workers (11.8 percent), and laborers except farm and mine (11 percent). On the other hand, clerical workers, who include many low-wage workers, have as low a rate of activity limitation as professional and technical workers (7.2 percent), reflecting not so much the better health of the group as the lower physical standards for their occupations.

Although there is essentially no difference between the employed and the unemployed in the prevalence of chronic health conditions (52 percent for both groups), there is a significant difference in severity, as indicated by limitation in ability to carry on their major economic activity, which affected 7 percent of the employed and 12.5 percent of the unemployed. The number of days during the year in which workers had to reduce their normal activity was 11.7 for the employed, 21.6 for the unemployed.

Differences in health are more marked between those in and those not in the labor force. For example, 48.1 percent of males aged 25–44 not in the labor force in 1964–65 had some disability imposing work limitation; the figure for employed males was 4.2 percent and for unemployed, 12.5 percent. The differences are much smaller for women.[57]

Of the total number of disabled workers receiving compensation in 1966 (only 8 percent of

whom were in the labor force), a high proportion
were employed in low-wage occupations at the
onset of their disability. Since low-wage workers
are incompletely covered under disability compensation, figures on beneficiaries understate the
concentration of disability among low-wage
workers. But statistics on severely disabled nonbe-
neficiaries (71 percent of whom were employed
before the onset of their disability) correct for this
as shown in Table 11. In 1966 the disabled had a
median education of eight years—four years less

TABLE 11
OCCUPATIONAL DISTRIBUTION OF
DISABLED WORKERS

Occupation at onset of disability	Total disabled worker beneficiaries	Severely disabled nonbeneficiaries
Professional and technical	3	6
Managers and officials	6	5
Clerical	8	6
Sales	3	5
Crafts	22	9
Operatives	31	23
Farm managers	3	3
Farm laborers	3	5
Private household	2	11
Service	9	14
Laborers	9	7
Not reported	2	7

SOURCE: *Health Insurance Disability Under
Social Security, 1969*, U.S. Advisory Council on
Health Insurance for the Disabled, appendix B,
Table A.

than the average, with 77 percent having less than a high school education. Nonwhites were 14 percent of the disabled, and 22 percent of the severely disabled—the last an overrepresentation by a factor of two which does not allow for the younger age structure of the nonwhite population. Forty-two percent of the severely disabled were from the South.[58]

The percentage of males not in the labor force in 1968 who gave poor health and/or disability as the reason was 29.3 for the 25–34 age group, but rose to 56.6 and 61.7 in the next two age groups, declining thereafter as retirement became a major reason. For women, the percentage attributing nonparticipation to ill health or disability also rises with age, but is never higher than 8.4 percent. A much higher percentage of nonwhites than of whites report ill health as their reason for not being in the labor force for every age group and for both sexes.[59]

Since the dominant factor in disability rates is age, clearly disability is not a factor in explaining the low wages or high unemployment rates among teen-agers. Nor can it be regarded as a factor in explaining low wages among women. For women have about the same overall disability rates as men; their higher self-reported rates of severe disability are questioned. The most convincing evidence, however, is that there is little difference in disability rates for women in and not in the labor force.

Employed Negroes have a higher rate of activity limitations than whites, for both sexes and all ages. Their rates of bed disability and work loss are much higher. Unemployed Negroes, however, report lower rates of activity limitations, bed disability, and chronic conditions than unemployed whites.[60] That is, disability is a relatively less important factor in unemployment among nonwhites than among whites, although non-whites' overall disability rates are higher.

Disability is undoubtedly a factor in low educational achievement. Thus, disability is a factor in the concentration of the poorly-educated in occupations where given chronic conditions are more economically disabling. Furthermore, their low education affords them less occupational flexibility to circumvent the economic consequences of chronic conditions or high morbidity rates.

Chapter Four
FACTORS CONTRIBUTING TO LOW WAGES

Chapter 3 identified low-wage workers: their who, what, and where. It avoided explanation. This chapter asks why. If low productivity is a characteristic of individuals, then future reductions in the number of low productivity employment opportunities is a cause for alarm. On the other hand, if low productivity is a characteristic of jobs and industries, not of workers, then we can unreservedly rejoice in the expected future reduction in the number of such jobs.

Interindustry differences in occupational wages suggest some interindustry immobility of labor. The position of the low-wage worker—his earnings, his employment and unemployment experience, his labor force participation—can best be understood in terms of the demand for low-wage workers, their supply, and the functioning of the labor market for low-productivity workers.

61

The Demand for Low-Wage Workers

The observed labor market experience of low-wage workers might be attributed to a lack of demand for their services. But the differential experience of various groups among low-wage workers suggests a more complex explanation. To some extent, their differential experience is attributable to discrimination against them in the labor market, rather than to low productivity of the individuals or of the jobs.

Discrimination

All employers discriminate in hiring, training, and promoting employees. Some discrimination is clearly related to costs, productivity, and profitability. The objective of other discrimination is either unrelated to economic performance or is based on ignorance or misinformation about the prospective performance of the workers discriminated against. It is only the latter type of discrimination that concerns us.

Discrimination may be revealed in two main ways: low wages for a given occupation or low occupational attainment. The latter may be defined in terms of educational attainment as one proxy (although not the only proxy) for occupational qualification. With the narrowing of the gap between the educational attainment of workers in low-wage occupations and other workers, this proxy is becoming inadequate. Discrimination occurs long before entry into the labor market, and is partially responsible for low educational attainment and other poor qualifications. There is a logical circularity in using one consequence of discrimination as an indicator of discrimination. However, this analysis must be limited to labor market discrimination.

Discrimination is not limited to low-wage occupations and industries. On the contrary, it appears to be greater in highly skilled occupations and may be absent in many low-skill occupations. By denying job and training opportunities in skilled occupations, it may crowd low-productivity occupations and industries with over-qualified workers and thereby exert downward pressure on earnings.

The impact of discrimination cannot be measured precisely by contrasting the occupational distribution of the group discriminated against and the rest of the labor force. For one thing, the implicit assumption that occupational, educational, and other preferences pertinent to occupational distribution of groups suffering from discrimination are the same as those of the rest of the labor force cannot be accepted. Women certainly have preferences that are different from those of men as a result of their potential role as mothers, if for no other reason. Discrimination may also be expected to affect labor force participation rates, particularly among women. It may raise unemployment rates.

Finally, if the group being discriminated against is large, as is true of Negroes and women, the discriminating group derives considerable advantage therefrom. A higher proportion of whites, and of males, is in professional and technical occupations by virtue of the handicaps which Negroes, and women, confront in seeking such jobs.[1]

The assumption above is that the occupational structure of the employed labor force is given, and elimination of discrimination will downgrade relatively many whites, and males, while it upgrades nonwhites and females.

The Equal Employment Opportunity Commission concluded, on the basis of its survey covering 26 million workers, that the lower educational attainment of Negroes accounted for only one-third of the difference in occupational rank between Negroes and anglos (that is, whites excluding individuals with Spanish surnames). Denoting this residual difference a measure of discrimination, "deliberate or inadvertent," the commission found that it is strongest in industries which (1) have a high proportion of Negroes; (2) have a high proportion of their operations in the South; (3) have a high proportion of well-paying positions; and (4) have Negro and white employees with a high average educational level.[2]

Earlier, Becker had reached similar conclusions: that discrimination seemed greater against the better-educated Negroes, and that perhaps there was a positive correlation between occupational rank and discrimination. He suggested that the difference in quality of schooling received by Negroes versus whites had a greater effect on differential income the higher the level of education attained. He also found that the educational and income differentials were largest in metropolitan areas with the highest proportion of Negroes.[3]

Hamel calculated that less than one-third of the nonwhite underrepresentation in white collar and craftsmen jobs could be attributed to lower educational attainment. The remainder he attributed to discrimination, inferior quality of education, lack of capital to enter business, and inability to obtain jobs commensurate with educational level.

It is difficult to evaluate the unemployment rate differential between Negroes and whites as an indicant of discrimination. As Killingsworth has pointed out, adjustment for male Negro underparticipation in the labor force raises the differential from 2:1 to nearly 3:1.[4] The Negro rates are higher for all ages and all levels of education except the lowest: four years of school or less (predominantly older workers, many in agriculture). This large unemployment rate differential developed during the 1950s, a period when Negro relative occupational position was improving, and persisted despite rapid gains in education, antidiscrimination laws, tight labor markets, etc.

Gilman attempts to measure the extent to which unemployment rate differentials reflect discrimination by standardizing for levels of skill.[5] He in this way eliminates half of the difference in unemployment rates between whites and nonwhites. In the South, the difference is eliminated altogether at low skill levels. In the non-South, the difference declines as skill increases, but remains substantially greater than in the South. Unless it is maintained that discrimination is substantially greater in the non-South, unemployment rates standardized for skill lack plausibility as adequate measures of discrimination.

Women are discriminated against for what seem to be entirely valid economic reasons. Statistically speaking, their attachment to the labor force is weaker, less permanent. Their prospect of turnover is higher. Therefore, insofar as potential for training and promotion is involved in the hiring decision, employers have an economic basis for discriminating against women in hiring. Insofar as turnover costs are high apart from training and promotion, again employers seem to discriminate rationally.

The evidence presented in chapter 3 makes it clear that women earn less than men in the same detailed occupation and with the same level of education. Quite apart from any discrimination in occupational choice and occupational entry and employment, this fact would appear to offer conclusive evidence of discrimination. This conclusion is not correct, however. Occupational earnings vary with the age of the worker. This variation simply reflects the underlying relation between occupational earnings and occupational experience. But women workers on the average are slightly younger than men workers; at the same age, women workers will have less work experience and less experience in their occupations (excepting the female-dominated occupations) than men. It is necessary to adjust for the sex difference in age and particularly in the age–experience relationship to determine what residual occupational earnings differential might be reasonably attributed to sex discrimination. Fuchs found that women earned 82 percent of male earnings after adjusting for age, education, race, and city size.[6] This does not allow for differences in the age–experience relation.

The assumption in much of the discussion above is that discrimination is by employers. Fuchs discounts this. Sanborn concludes that consumer discrimination and coworker discrimination are more important than employer discrimination.[7]

It is difficult to ascertain the influence of these economic considerations on the lower occupational position of women and on their lower earnings within occupations. In establishments employing women exclusively, however, objections to hiring and promoting women are invalid. Yet where establishments in the same industry, or the same locality, have been compared, those employing women exclusively have wages well below those employing both sexes or men exclusively. The differences in wages between men and women in establishments employing both are small.[8] The fact that establishments coexist with widely different sex ratios by occupation, and with widely different average earnings of women, strongly suggests discrimination. But without assurance that there are no compensating factors, such as differences in productivity, the evidence is not conclusive.

There is labor market discrimination at both ends of the age spectrum, but in terms of low-wage workers it is discrimination against the very young

that matters. A study conducted for the National
Committee on Employment of Youth determined
that employers discriminated against the very
young in a variety of ways. The most direct was an
unwillingness to hire teen-agers. Of employers
surveyed, 18 percent never or rarely hired workers
under twenty-one; 34 percent required that entry
workers be eighteen years old or high school
graduates.[9] This policy was explained in terms of
irresponsibility, instability, high turnover of very
young male workers. (High turnover was accepted
for females.) More frequent was stress on experience. Occupational experience was regarded as a
rough indication of labor quality. Half the employers surveyed required experience for some
jobs. A high school diploma for all jobs was
required by 20 percent of the smaller firms and 29
percent of the larger firms. This stress is related to
employer judgment of "trainability." The reason
for regarding some of the stress on experience and
high school graduation as unjustified is that they
are demanded for many jobs that require no
previous experience and for many jobs that are not
the first rung on any occupational ladder.

Diamond and Bedrosian studied industry
hiring requirements from the viewpoint of disadvantaged groups.[10] They concluded that overstated
hiring requirements were a major cause of high
turnover, which sometimes coexisted with labor
shortages. The great majority of industry respondents refused to consider applicants under twenty-
one years of age, although no significant correla-
tions were found between age and measures of job

performance. Most industries had quite specific educational requirements, although these varied widely. Promotion potential was stressed by the majority of employers in most occupations, although the possibilities for promotion in the occupations involved were usually less than one in ten over a two-year period. Experience was almost universally desired, even where training periods were measured in weeks. The great majority of employers also had marked preferences with regard to appearance and worker traits.

What is striking about the findings is the considerable differences among respondents in the level of requirements they specify and in the reasons they have for stressing particular criteria. Furthermore, employers, with rare exceptions, do not check job performance against their hiring criteria.

The United States Employment Service estimated minimum general education and specific vocational preparation requirements for 4,000 jobs in 1956 (largely basing them on its experience with employers). These requirements exceeded the median education in 1960 in 47 percent of the occupations with 30 percent of the employment.[11] Most of the large discrepancies were in low-wage occupations. Given the dramatic increase in the median educational attainment of younger members of the labor force, it is not surprising that entry educational requirements for many occupations should be higher than the median attainment of those already working in the occupation. This reflects the increased availability, say, of high school graduates and the need to upgrade educational criteria if they are to serve any selective purpose.

Hiring practices favoring the more educated, experienced, and older youth, or favoring males, are useful for selecting among job candidates. Employers show considerable flexibility in moderating their requirements when faced with a shortage of applicants meeting their listed criteria. Available evidence, with the exception of evidence regarding discrimination against Negroes, does not permit a quantitative judgment of where relevant selection procedures shade into unjustified discrimination.

Demand for Low-Skill Occupations

The extent and impact of discrimination decline in a tight labor market. The demand for low-skill labor, therefore, is both a direct determinant of employment and wages and an indirect influence on opportunities for specific low-wage groups. What is happening to this demand, and what is likely to happen in the future?

Demand can be considered in terms of employment trends of low-wage occupations; trends in skill levels of occupational groups; and employment trends in low-wage industries. These trends are not direct observations of demand, but are direct observations of the market outcome of various forces in which demand is a major, if not the dominant, influence.

The fate of the occupational groups including

the bulk of low-wage workers has proved mixed in the past, and promises to remain mixed. Although the relative and absolute decline in farm employment and in private household employment is expected to continue, the base is now so much smaller that the reduction in jobs will be less. Service workers, however, are the only group in which substantial absolute increases in employment can be expected.

The common view that technological progress is eliminating employment opportunities for unskilled and semiskilled workers is vastly exaggerated if not altogether wrong. James Bright does not believe that automation means lack of opportunity

TABLE 12
PERCENTAGE OF EMPLOYMENT
IN
LOW-WAGE OCCUPATIONS

	1960	1970	1980
Clerical	14.8	17.4	18.2
Sales	6.4	6.2	6.3
Operatives	18.2	17.7	16.2
Laborers except farm	5.4	4.7	3.7
Service workers*	12.2	12.4	13.8
Farmers and farm laborers	7.9	4.0	2.7

SOURCE: *Manpower Report of the President*, 1973, p. 225.

*Including private household workers

for the unskilled worker. He finds that the net effect of automation in most plants is "to reduce, or at least not to increase ... the demand for skills and abilities of the direct labor force." Ewan Clague concludes: "My own judgment is that on balance, the trend of skills is upward, but I do not have the analytical data with which to answer this question with certainty."[12]

Scoville evaluated general educational development and specific vocational preparation requirements for a large number of specific occupations. He concluded that requirements for education have risen 4.4 percent and for vocational preparation 7.7 percent since 1940, with most of the increases being post-1950.[13] Most, if not all, of this increase in aggregate requirements levels stems from shifts in the relative proportions of major occupational groups. The only low-wage occupational group for which there has been a perceptible increase in educational and vocational requirements is farm laborers and foremen.

Raimon and Stoikov arrive at similar conclusions from a different point of departure.[14] They attempt to measure changes in the quality of the labor force, using median earnings of full-time workers as occupational quality weights. Their conclusion is that the quality of the employed labor force rose only 0.72 percent between 1956 and 1964, and the quality of the unemployed has been falling since 1960, excluding agriculture. Including agriculture, quality of the employed has increased 2.75 percent. Little further increase in quality is expected by 1975.

Killingsworth estimates demand trends (measured by employment) for low-skill workers as measured by their educational attainment.[15] He found a pronounced decline in demand for workers with less than five years of education at a 3.5 percent annual rate between 1950 and 1962 and at a 5 percent rate between 1962 and 1967. Demand for workers with 5–8 years of schooling also declined, but at a much lower rate. On the other hand, demand for workers with 9–11 years of schooling increased slightly between 1962 and 1967.

Technological Progress and Employment in Low-Wage Industries

Ultimately, the demand for low-skill labor and the occupational mix of the employed is dependent on the changing interindustry composition of the national economy and on the changing industry production techniques. Of the two, industry changes in unit labor requirements are more likely to affect industry demand for low-skill labor than are interindustry changes in the structure of demand.[16]

Technological change can be expected to continue at an unabated, if not accelerated, pace in the years ahead. For, expenditures on research and development (R&D) increased almost exponentially throughout the late 1950s and early 1960s. In current dollar terms, expenditures increased tenfold in about 15 years. Since there are generally long lags between initiation of research and com-

mercial production, and since much of the increase
in research was not directly oriented toward commercial objectives, involving additional lags, it can
be expected that many of the economic consequences of this revolutionary increase in R&D are
still ahead.

The prospects for employment of low-skill,
low-wage workers, however, do not depend solely
on the net effects of technological change on the
skill mix. They depend on the gross effects: new
low-skill jobs are being created to replace higher-
skill jobs eliminated by automation at the same
time that old low-skill jobs are eliminated elsewhere by technological progress. Accelerated
change, even without net effects on the demand for
skill, requires accelerated mobility on the part of
workers if they are to maintain their current rates
of employment. Mobility may be between firms,
industries, occupations, or locations. For low-skill
workers, presumably a great deal of training and
retraining is not involved, although it may well be
required to maintain the earnings of higher-skill
workers. Possible adverse effects of rapid technological change on low-wage workers, then, issue
both from the elimination of low-skill jobs and
from the requirement of mobility from a sector of
the labor force whose mobility is relatively low.
Adjustment needs are accentuated by major shifts
in the sex composition of low-wage industry employment (mainly the shift from agriculture to
trade and services). These shifts in sex composition
also involve shifts from export to local market
industry and their associated geographical redistribution of low-wage employment opportunities.

TABLE 13
EMPLOYMENT IN LOW-WAGE INDUSTRIES
(1,000s)

	1959	1971	1980
Agriculture	5,564	3,387	3,000
Textiles	946	957	
Apparel	1,226	1,336	
Lumber and wood products	659	581	
Furniture and fixtures	385	458	
Leather and leather products	374	302	
Rubber and miscellaneous products	373	581	
Miscellaneous manufacturing	388	410	
Retail trade	8,182	11,333	16,090
Services	7,130	11,869	13,025

SOURCES: *1969 Business Statistics* (Supplement to the *Survey of Current Business*), pp. 69–71, and *Survey of Current Business*, October 1972; for 1980, *Manpower Report of the President*, 1972, p. 259.

As noted before, the greatest concentration of low-wage workers is in the local market industries, not in the "export" industries, excepting agriculture and hotels and other lodging places. It is in retail trade, in hospitals, in private households, in various service industries. The direct impact of technical change on low-wage workers is not through the progress of the economy at large, but through developments in low-wage industries. These industries can be subdivided into services, trade, manufacturing, and agriculture.

In services, the evidence is that their productivity gains, in general, have lagged—low-wage services in particular.[17] Slower productivity gains mean that the price of services has risen relative to the price of goods. Income elasticity of demand of about 1.12 means that as incomes rise, a larger share of income is spent on services.[18] With slower gains in productivity accounting largely for the rise in the relative price of services, employment in services tends to rise. This is not true of all services. Health and medical care, education, tourism, and recreation and travel seem to be major beneficiaries, whereas laundry and cleaning establishments (although growing slowly) have suffered from a number of innovations in other industries: a combination of household capital equipment and new textile fibers and new finishes. The motion pictures industry has declined in employment because of development of new substitutes (TV). So, the slow reduction in the low-skill occupation share in service industries may be counteracted by services' increased share of aggregate employment.

Demand for goods is slightly less elastic than demand for services. Hence, retail trade, more than services, has depended for its increased share of employment on its slow growth of productivity relative to the growth of productivity in goods-producing industry. Retail trade is subject to diverse influences of concentration and dispersion with the changing urban geography of residence, employment, and transportation. But in the near future there seems no prospect of a diminished demand for low-skill workers and for part-time workers. Because of retail trade's substantial sea-sonality, there will be no decrease in opportunities for temporary work.

In agriculture and the low-wage manufac-turing industries, policy variables may prove more important than technology or demand. Agriculture has experienced rapid technological progress which, in combination with the very low income elasticity of demand for food products (although not for all of them), has led to a steady decline in its share of aggregate demand. A low price elas-ticity of demand has limited the growth of sales also. Yet American farmers could expand export sales at competitive prices in many products were it not for protective policies in Europe and else-where. Present world shortages are temporary.

Low-wage manufacturing industries have ex-perienced faster than average productivity gains.[19] Nevertheless, employment in textiles and apparel, which account for half the manufacturing employ-ment in low-wage three-digit industries, is a function of the level of protection from imports. To a lesser extent, this is true of many other low-wage industries: lumber and wood products, miscella-neous manufacturing, miscellaneous plastics prod-ucts, and leather products.

The contrast in net trade position between low-wage and high-wage manufacturing industries makes it evident that the prospects for low-wage employment in manufacturing are poor. The rela-tive growth of industries such as apparel, because of their slower productivity gain in combination with perhaps an income-elastic (and a price-inelastic) demand for their products, is conditional on ever higher import barriers.

Our fundamental concern, however, is not with employment trends and prospects in low-wage industries, but with why they are low-wage. Although the composition of low-wage industries has shown considerable stability, it is not immutable. What makes an industry an employer of low-skill workers, a low-wage activity?

Characteristics of Low-Wage Industries

Low-wage industry is typically highly competitive, with many small firms producing very similar products or services. Firms are not only small in absolute terms, but are small relative to their markets. Agriculture most nearly approximates the simple model of perfect competition. In low-wage manufacturing, the number of firms is large, concentration ratios typically are low, and markets are national. In trade and services, firms are even smaller than in manufacturing, but markets are mainly local. Even when firms are large, however, establishments are small, and it is the local establishment rather than the national firm that is of greatest relevance for low-wage workers. In many cases, particularly in smaller towns, some firms (establishments) will have monopoly power, but power strictly limited in degree and in reach.

On a priori grounds, therefore, it does not seem plausible to explain low wages on the basis of the exploitation of labor. Few firms in low-wage industries are likely to be dominant in any local labor market, with the exceptions being in the smaller towns. The correlation between wage rates and concentration in manufacturing is low.[20] In trade and services, local wage patterns are likely to be influenced by export industries. Empirically, the profits of low-wage industries are lower than the average. Most of the labor in the lowest-wage industry, agriculture, is self-employed, hence any exploitation must be by monopsonist buyers of farm products, but, again, the consuming industries exhibit typically high competition and low concentration. Certainly, exploitation cannot serve as a general explanation for low wages.

Low wages (or large interindustry differentials) might be accounted for, in part, by lack of competition in high-wage industries. Fuchs compared the actual earnings in 138 industries with earnings to be expected on the basis of age, sex, race, and educational attainment of their employees.[21] In manufacturing, earnings were higher than expected, except in lumber and wood products, furniture and fixtures, pottery and related products, leather products, and several, but not all, food products and textile mill products industries. The one important low-wage industry where earnings were higher than expected was apparel and accessories. On the other hand, all lines of retail trade had earnings below expectations, as did all types of personal services identified and hospitals. In many cases, actual earnings were far below expected earnings. Fuchs concluded that two-thirds of the earnings differential between industry and services was explained by the degree of unionization. (Services as a whole was only ten percent unionized.) Establishment size was the second most important explanatory variable.

Competitive industries paying low wages and making low profits lack the ability to pay high wages. Their productivity per worker must be low, and they employ a high proportion of low-skill workers. One may infer that such industries have little capital per worker compared to high-wage industries, and that they are labor-intensive.[22] Estimates on capital investment lack the desired industry detail, but, in general, strongly support the above conclusion. Hickman estimated the net depreciated value of plant and equipment in manufacturing and petroleum extraction at $100.4 billion in 1962. The total for textiles was $4.3 billion and for rubber and miscellaneous plastics products, $1.2 billion. For all other nondurables (including the largely low-wage printing industries) the total was $3.7 billion.[23] Furthermore, the new investment per worker in low-wage industries is low relative to higher-wage industries, despite the fact that the former's productivity gains are slightly higher.[24] For trade and services as a whole, both capital per worker and new investment per worker fall well below the manufacturing average. There are no breakdowns, however, to distinguish between the low-wage and higher-wage trade and service industries.

One might also expect industries that are persistently low-wage to be characterized by low rates of increase in productivity. These expectations are only partially fulfilled. Agriculture has been gaining rapidly in productivity. Among manufacturing industries, the low-wage industries have gained in productivity somewhat faster than the others.[25] Services have lagged far behind industry in productivity gains, and within services, the lowest-wage seems to have lagged more than the higher-wage (for many services there are no estimates of productivity because of difficulty in measuring output). The same conclusions about low productivity gains apply to retail trade.[26]

All low-wage industries have done poorly in terms of research and development expenditures, whether these are expressed in dollars per employee, by a percentage of value added, or by a percentage of sales. Of $17,858 million spent by industry on research and development in 1970, textiles and apparel spent a combined total of $64 million and lumber, wood products, and furniture spent only $24 million.[27] All trade and services and other nonmanufacturing activities combined spent $669 million. As indicated above, however, some industries, benefitting from research in other industries, have advanced rapidly in productivity nevertheless. Farming productivity gains result from research by government, universities and various industries supplying inputs of farmers. Textiles have advanced substantially thanks to research and development by chemicals and machinery industries. There is little relation, then, between research intensity and productivity gains on an industry by industry basis. Furthermore, there is little relation between rates of change in hourly earnings and in industry productivity.[28]

TABLE 14
AVERAGE CYCLICAL CHANGE OF
EMPLOYMENT
NET OF TREND, 1947–65
(Percent Per Annum)

Total nonagricultural employment	6.4
Manufacturing	13.3
Durables	19.8
Nondurables	5.0
Retail trade	2.8
Services	1.6

SOURCE: Victor R. Fuchs, *The Service Economy* (New York: National Bureau of Economic Research, 1968), pp. 166–167, 169.

Low-wage workers also experience above-average unemployment rates. This experience must be attributable either to the individuals themselves or to the industries in which they are concentrated. High unemployment among low-wage workers cannot be attributed to their concentration in industries with wide cyclical fluctuations in employment. Retail trade and the low-wage services show much less cyclical variation than the economy as a whole. The low-wage manufacturing industries are predominantly in nondurable manufacturing which is less cyclically sensitive than durables manufacturing.

TABLE 15
SEASONALITY OF EMPLOYMENT BY
INDUSTRY, 1969

Industry	Seasonality Index
All manufacturing (unweighted average, 2-digit industries)	1.05
Food and kindred products	1.13
Tobacco manufactures	1.36
Textile mill products	1.02
Apparel	1.03
Lumber and wood products	1.08
Furniture and fixtures	1.03
Rubber and miscellaneous plastics products	1.03
Leather and leather products	1.09
Miscellaneous manufacturing industries	1.11
Retail trade	1.11
Services	1.04
Hotels and other lodging places	1.27
Personal services	1.03
Medical and health services	1.02

SOURCE: Calculated from *Employment and Earnings,* U.S. Department of Labor, Bureau of Labor Statistics, June 1970, p. 120.

On the other hand, low-wage industries exhibit more seasonal fluctuation in number of employees than the economy as a whole. This is notably true of agriculture. In manufacturing, the most seasonal industries are predominantly low-wage: fruit and vegetable and seafood canning, cigars, lumber and wood products, toys and sporting goods (in miscellaneous manufacturing industries). Retail trade is more seasonal than manufacturing. Although services as a whole are not very seasonal, some of the low-wage services, e.g., hotels and other lodging places, are highly seasonal. Table 15 presents an index calculated by dividing employment in the peak month by employment in the trough month for major groups with important low-wage industry components. Low-wage workers experience higher rates of seasonal unemployment which affect annual earnings rather than wage rates. In trade and services, these inferences are partially invalidated by the use of temporary workers.

The Supply of Low-Skill Labor

Trends in demand for low-wage low-skill labor mean nothing by themselves. They must be related to changes in supply before any inferences are possible about the consequences for low-skill workers or about policy recommendations. Strictly speaking, there is no demand for low-productivity workers. There is a demand for labor, which is an inverse function of wages, and an ability to use low-skill labor profitably.

Supply has been the great underlying influence on the wages and unemployment experience of low-skill workers in the last generation, that is, the movement of many millions from rural areas to the cities.[29] Ten million people migrated in the decade of the 1950s alone. Agricultural employment declined from 7.9 million in 1947 to 3.4 million in 1971. This movement has been accompanied by increases in birthrates which have had a delayed impact on the labor market until the 1960s and later.

These developments increasing the supply of urban low-wage labor were counteracted, to some extent, by the rapid increase in the educational attainment of the labor force as a high school diploma became the rule for the young generation.

The consequences to be expected in the nonagricultural labor market include a widening of the wage differential between skilled and unskilled workers.

In addition to these general trends, more specific supply effects possibly affecting the unemployment and wages of low-productivity workers include (1) commuters across the Mexican border; (2) foreign farm workers; (3) migration of Puerto Ricans, mainly to New York; and (4) immigration of Cubans, mainly to Miami.

Labor Force Participation and Attachment

The increase in the supply of low-skill nonfarm labor has been accompanied by a change in its character. Much of the net increase in the labor force has consisted of a sharp rise in female labor force participation. The labor force participation of many women is less autonomous than that of men. It responds to the number and quality of employment opportunities;[30] demand creates its own supply. Second, many women want part-time work, or want work for only part of the year. This perhaps makes the matching of labor demand and supply more difficult. The increase in the percentage of very young age groups in the labor force also contributes toward reducing attachment to the labor force. The increase in the share of both of these groups should have adversely affected their relative positions in terms of unemployment rates and earnings.

The evidence on the labor force participation of women is contradictory. It is higher for Negroes than for whites, reflecting greater economic need and high unemployment for men. But even for Negro women living in poverty areas, there is evidence that the participation rate is held down by lack of jobs or by the belief that jobs are not obtainable. On this basis, improvement of economic conditions associated with increased employment opportunities would increase participation in the short run, but would reduce it, due to improved income, in the longer run. On the other hand, there is a clear trend for increased married female labor force participation, once children are in school, or grown. This tendency is positively related to education and also to the husband's income well beyond the poverty line.[31] Wives with some college have a higher labor force participation if they have no children under 18, and especially none under 6, than if they do. By contrast, wives with eight or fewer years of school experience their highest labor force participation when they have children aged 6–17. There is no way, at present, to assess the conflicting trends and strike a balance.

The increase in labor force participation of

women, considering their occupational concentration, should have depressed their earnings relative to those of men. The high proportion of women who work part-time (30 percent of all women with work experience in 1968)[32] is a further depressing factor, both because of the rapid increase in the supply of part-time labor and because opportunities for part-time employment are concentrated in retail trade (30 percent of workers in retail trade work less than thirty-five hours a week) and low-wage services. By contrast, only 11.3 percent of males had part-time jobs in 1968. Females accounted for 11 of 17 million part-time workers. Furthermore, there is a high correlation between part-time work and work for less than the full year. Only one-third of the part-time female workers were employed for the full year and nearly half worked for less than twenty-six weeks. On the other hand, four-sevenths of full-time female workers were employed for the full year.

The same trends should have raised the unemployment rate differentials between men and women. The unemployment rate for part-time workers was 6.5 percent in 1969, more than twice that for full-time workers, and higher than the 4.7 rate for all females. Other factors relating to the labor force attachment of women, however, probably account for most of the observed differential. Many women withdraw and reenter the labor force more than once. The median number of years women had been in their current job in January 1968 was only half the number for men (excluding the 16–24 age group).[33]

A survey of married women who started working in 1963 provided additional information on the nature of their labor force attachment.[34] Financial necessity was given as the most important reason by 41.6 percent, but by 45 percent of women with less than a high school education, and by 59.5 percent of women whose husbands earned less than $60 a week. However, 56 percent stated that they preferred to work and would not stop working if money were no longer needed. Personal satisfaction was given by 19 percent and was directly related to educational attainment and particularly to the husband's income. Slightly more than half the wives, whatever their reason for working, preferred full-time work to part-time work.

The somewhat weaker or more temporary attachment of many women than of men to the labor force means that a larger share of female than male response to changing labor market conditions takes the form of withdrawal and reentry into the labor market, rather than affecting unemployment rates.[35]

The labor force participation rate of teen-age males has dropped because of increased school enrollment. Female teen-ager participation rates, however, have shown no trend. The total teen-age labor force jumped from 4.7 million in 1949 to 8.4 million in 1972.[36] A rising proportion, however, were temporary entrants who continued their schooling. The median job tenure for all workers aged 16 through 24 was only 0.7 years and,

undoubtedly, significantly less for teen-agers.[37]
The high teen-ager unemployment rate is not
explainable in terms of rates of job loss or of
voluntary job-leaving, although both rates, especially quits, are higher than those of adults.[38] In
1968, entrants accounted for 39.4 percent of the
unemployment of 16–19-year-olds, and reentrants
accounted for another 33.5 percent. Their elimination would have reduced the 12.7 percent unemployment rate to a modest 3.3 percent.

The increase in the teen-ager share of the
labor force was reflected in rising unemployment
rate differentials, partly because of wage inflexibility which precluded adjustment via wider wage
differentials between teen-agers and older
workers.[39] Brozen has found that federal minimum
wage legislation, by reducing wage differentials
temporarily every time the minimum is raised,
increases temporarily the unemployment rate differentials between teen-agers and the total labor
force.[40]

In sum, two largely low-wage components of
the labor force, women and teen-agers, have
increased sharply as a percentage of the total. They
are characterized by a relatively weak attachment
to the labor force, with short job tenure, high
incidence of part-time work, and high turnover.
Low annual earnings reflect these characteristics
(which are largely a matter of voluntary preference) as well as low wage rates. With labor force
participation partly optional, unemployment rates
are poor indicants of labor market performance.

Nevertheless, the relative increase in these groups tends to raise their relative unemployment rates and depress their relative wages.

The labor force participation rate for men of all ages has declined slightly. Single men reveal rates far below those of married men. In 1971, the participation rate was 84.4 percent for single men aged 25–34 (the age group with the highest rate) and 97.8 percent for married men.[41] Much of this differential is explainable in terms of disability, higher among single men. But disability cannot explain the decline in rates for single men. Evidence that some of this decline represents an increasingly discretionary participation . includes the fact that: one-fifth of single men were on voluntary part-time in 1969, contrasted to one-tenth of married men; the decline occurred in a period when unemployment rates were falling; and, most men not in the labor force have worked in the recent past, and plan to seek work in the near future.[42]

The rise in nonparticipation among males not enrolled in school is particularly notable among young Negroes. Men not in the labor force are not only disproportionately nonwhite, but disproportionately are concentrated in lower-wage occupations. Many represent a "discouraged worker" response to prolonged unemployment, and only one-third of these discouraged nonparticipants had a high school education.[43] "Discretionary" and "discouraged" workers overlap, and where to draw the line we do not know.

In estimating the supply of low-skill labor, it is

not sufficient to count hands. As indicated before, 30 percent of employed women work part time by choice, and nearly half the married women in the labor force would prefer to work part time. At the other extreme, there were 3.6 million workers, predominantly male, holding two or more jobs in May 1966.[44] Moonlighting rates are inversely related to earnings in the primary job and are directly related to the number of children under eighteen. By occupation, the highest moonlighting rates are for farmers and farm managers and service workers (protective service workers have an especially high rate). Sixteen percent of secondary jobs are farming and farm management. The data on dual jobholding, however, are no measure of the available labor supply; they are an indication of employment opportunities in secondary jobs, constrained as they are by primary job work schedules. Presumptive evidence that there is an excess supply of labor willing to work more than one full-time job includes the underrepresentation of Negroes among moonlighters, despite their lower earnings in primary jobs, and the willingness of many workers to work overtime (a willingness, however, often accentuated by premium pay rates or assured by contract).

Alien Commuters and Immigrants

International commuting as well as immigration of labor have been cited as threats to the pay and employment prospects of low-productivity workers. Surveys of communities near the Mexican border that have a considerable proportion of cross-border commuters in their labor force reveal both lower wages by sectors and broad occupational groups and higher unemployment than the state as a whole.[45] These findings are inconclusive because other communities farther from the border and not dependent upon immigrant labor have lower wages for some occupational groups, and the border communities are depressed in many cases and might reveal the same findings even without cross-border commuters. More conclusive is comparison of establishments in the same industry employing aliens and citizens. The former invariably have lower wages, usually by a large margin.[46]

The total number of "green card" commuters, that is, aliens who have met immigration requirements but are living in Mexico while working in the U.S., was only 49,770 in December 1969. An estimated 20,000 U.S. citizens were living in Mexico and working in the United States.[47] The problem is clearly very small, limited to a few border communities and, except in El Paso, Laredo, Cordova, Nogales, and Brownsville, concentrated in agricultural hired labor.

Immigrant workers, with certain exceptions, must be certified for admission. Certification involves ascertaining that their employment would not affect wages or working conditions adversely for domestic workers. The number of immigrants approved for permanent employment in fiscal year 1967 was 93,324.[48] Most of the low-wage workers approved were service workers (34,336), preponderantly live-in maids. One-third of the approved service workers in fiscal year 1967 intended to reside in New York. California and New Jersey together accounted for over 20 percent.[49] These figures overstate the potential impact on low-productivity workers for two reasons: they are gross, and should be deflated for immigrants returning home; they do not allow for the fact that quite a few workers entering in low-productivity jobs quickly move up. These figures understate the magnitude of the problem of immigrant workers since they exclude aliens working illegally (a number much reduced since extension of the Fair Labor Standards Act to most agricultural hired workers and since the 1964 enactment of U.S.–Mexican regulation of imported seasonal agricultural labor). Aliens working illegally, preponderantly in low-wage jobs, may pose a greater threat to jobs and wages than aliens holding work permits. Their numbers, although unknown, are estimated to be well into the six figures. Nevertheless, the total number of immigrant alien workers entering the United States is too small a proportion of the labor force, or even of the net annual increment in the labor force, to affect the conditions of low-productivity workers in general, although in particular areas, industries and occupations, alien workers may brake wage increases.

Alien farm workers present a special case because the preponderance are not immigrants, but temporary visitors working by the season, and because of their geographical concentration. Before the termination of the bracero program in 1964, Mexicans were a significant part of the agricultural labor force in the Western United States, and they were a factor in keeping down wages and working conditions. Since 1964, farm workers can only be brought in under the same conditions as any other workers—after assurances that their prospective employer has made reasonable efforts to recruit domestic workers and that foreign workers would not adversely affect the wages of domestic workers. The amendment of the Fair Labor Standards Act to cover some farm laborers in 1961, the later extension to cover most farm laborers, and staged increases in minimum wages toward the $1.60 minimum, all have reduced the incentives to import foreign farm labor and have diminished the threat to wages and employment of domestic workers. In fact, the annual number of foreign farm workers admitted for temporary agricultural employment has dropped from an average of 400,000 in 1955–59 to 200,000 in 1964, less than 36,000 in 1965, and less than 24,000 in each of the next two years.[50]

The decline in dependence on foreign agricultural workers thus preceded the end of the bracero program. It accelerated a process already going on: the substitution of capital for labor. As long as cheap foreign labor was available, mechanization was held back. As this labor became more expensive, substitution took place, even before the supply was sharply curtailed. Between 1959 and 1964 the dependence on foreign agricultural labor had already fallen by more than half; in 1964 foreign labor was only 0.9 percent of agricultural labor and 7.5 percent of seasonal farm labor. Half of it, however, was in California (52.8 percent in 1964), 13.1 percent was in Texas, and 12.7 percent in Florida. The gain to domestic farm workers was therefore temporary and limited. Between 1964 and 1965, for instance, when foreign employment dropped by 43,700, domestic employment rose by only 11,800.[51]

The acid tests of the impact of immigration on low-wage workers are Miami and New York. Miami experienced a very large influx of Cubans in a short period of time, most of whom initially competed with citizens for low-wage, low-productivity jobs. The New York experience refers not to immigration (except in a much earlier period) but to Puerto Rican migrants since World War II. Coming from conditions of much higher unemployment, and much lower wages, they posed the same kind of threat to wage levels and employment prospects in New York that Mexican commuters pose for Texas border cities.

Fleischer studied the impact of Puerto Rican migration to New York City.[52] His findings were that it adversely affected Negro migration to New York City; it was partially responsible for a slower rate of growth in average hourly wages in the apparel industry in New York City than in the country as a whole. The main determinant of industry behavior, however, was demand, which was expanding throughout the period of high migration. There are no studies of the impact of Puerto Rican migrants in the various local service industries where they are highly concentrated and in which they have become a significant proportion of the labor force.

Friedlander studied the period 1952–62.[53] He found that the unemployment rate of low-skill Puerto Ricans in New York City was higher than in Puerto Rico and much higher than that of migrants before they left Puerto Rico. His conclusion is that wage differentials, not differentials in prospect of employment, were responsible for the migration. He did not test for the impact on occupational or industry earnings. The data on unemployment, however, suggest that the Puerto Ricans themselves absorbed much of the impact of excess supply and that much of this impact was in the form of unemployment rather than lower wages or slower wage increases.[54]

No studies are known of the impact of Cubans on wage trends in Miami or on the migration of low-wage workers. However, starting with May 1962, Cuban refugees were included in the unemployment count. For some months two separate rates were available, showing that adding the Cubans raised the unemployment rate about three percentage points (implying an extremely high rate of unemployment for the Cubans at the time).[55] The rate remained over 8 percent most of the time until early 1964, but dropped below 4 percent by January 1965, and since then the rate has averaged below the national rate. In 1966 workers of Spanish surname accounted for about 13 percent of all employees in the Miami area in establishments reporting to the Equal Employment Opportunity Commission. They were still concentrated in low-wage industries, but their overrepresentation in low-wage occupational groups, and underrepresentation in high-wage occupational groups, was not very great.[56]

Behavioral Characteristics of Low-Skill Workers

A last factor bearing from the supply side on the experience of low-wage workers is the set of work attitudes and behavioral patterns that many low-skill workers bring to the labor market, adversely affecting their prospects for employment and income.

The attitudes can be described as a counter-discrimination, an unwillingness to accept menial, low-pay, dead-end, low-status jobs.[57] This attitude is largely a function of expectations. One factor in rising expectations of better employment is the rapid increase in educational attainment of young workers combined with society's unrelenting campaign that equates education with high income and attractive jobs. But the phenomenon of rising expectations is more widespread than this. A survey of educational and occupational aspirations found surprisingly little difference between families with an unskilled or semiskilled wage earner and a professional or managerial wage earner.[58] Eighty-eight percent of the former wanted college training for their children versus 98 percent of the latter. The corresponding figures for high-status occupational aspiration were 75 and 97 percent. The children were considerably less optimistic than the parents. But Negroes had aspirations significantly and consistently higher than whites.

Such expectations have consequences, for example, a withholding of labor from employment in
undesirable jobs by the significant number of
young people neither in school nor in the labor
force. This consequence is demonstrated by the
coexistence of high unemployment rates among
low-skill workers and many unfilled job openings
in the same localities with minimal entry requirements. It is demonstrated by the certification by
the Department of Labor of immigrants on a
permanent or temporary basis to fill such job
openings.

The wider availability of income without
work, whether in cash or in kind, provides at least
a temporary alternative to low-wage employment
and permits temporary indulgence of possibly
unrealistic expectations.

Leonard Goodwin has found approximately
the same attachment to work among recipients of
Aid to Families with Dependent Children as
among working members of the labor force.[59] The
issue, however, is not acceptance of the work
ethic; the issue is behavior patterns conducive to
getting and holding a job and attitudes not toward
work in the abstract, but toward particular employment opportunities which may be available. It is
highlighted by the following reactions to the new
"workfare" provisions requiring able-bodied welfare recipients under AFDC to register for work
and accept jobs as a condition of continuing
benefits. Beatrice Knight, director of the Midlands
Welfare Rights Organization in Columbus, South
Carolina, said recipients want jobs that provide a

measure of dignity. "We shall refuse to accept jobs as domestics, in either private homes or hotels or motels. We shall refuse to accept jobs as waitresses or food servers in either schools, restaurants, or hospitals."[60] A welfare recipient in California, which is experimenting with a program of unpaid work for a government or nonprofit agency as a condition of welfare payments for recipients not placed in jobs or training programs, expressed her feelings as follows: "It's a form of slavery. Either you go to work at a demeaning job or your children go hungry. Some choice."[61]

Behavioral patterns hampering employment, on the other hand, are alleged to derive from a "culture of poverty"[62] or a "lower class culture." The central trait characteristic of this culture is extreme present-orientation, or inability to defer gratification. Individuals of this culture are unwilling to complete high school, to undergo any extended training program, to plan, to consider the consequences of their behavior. They lack achievement motivation. They are unreliable, violence-prone, and fatalistic. Edward Banfield, in his recent book *The Unheavenly City*, emphasizes what he calls "the imperatives of class" in explaining the position of the poor in the labor force and the difficulties in improving their position.[63] He has been criticized for attributing the position of the Negro to his participation in a "lower class" subculture rather than to discrimination.

Most poor, most low-wage workers, are white; for them, Banfield's emphasis may not be misplaced. For the minority who are black, discrimination is an obstacle which hampers those who are not members of a lower class subculture, as well as those who are. Of course, the two factors reinforce each other. Discrimination breeds lower class attitudes and forces Negroes into jobs and environments where such a subculture is likely to flourish.

Piore describes the "secondary" labor market which operates largely in urban ghettos. High central-city rates of unemployment are symptomatic of the high turnover rate in this "secondary" labor market. Employment in this market is short term, unstable, lacking prospects, and inferior in pay and working conditions. It competes with welfare and illegal sources of income. Workers who have adapted to this market have great difficulty in fitting into the primary labor market because the two markets are associated with quite different behavioral requirements and conditioning. Specifically, employment in the secondary labor market does not require faithful attendance, does not punish tardiness, provides no formal grievance procedures, offers no prospects for continued employment or for advancement. Therefore, it engenders attitudes and behavior patterns inappropriate in the primary labor market. Piore is suggesting that rather than being the cause of an environment, a "culture of poverty" is induced by an environment.[64]

The nature of this culture of poverty is an unsettled issue.[65] Some have pointed out that if there is no expectation of gratification, there is nothing to defer. If there is no prospect for opportunity, or belief in it, there can be no achievement motivation. If present needs are urgent they will take precedence over future benefits: education, training, saving. An individual with little control over events and no feeling of control does not plan ahead. In brief, the culture of poverty is, as the name implies, an adaptation to an environment. It is not a set of values, attitudes, and behavior patterns that engenders unemployment and nonparticipation or limits skill, education, and initiative.

The inheritance of low skill can be argued to result from either an inheritance of cultural values or an inheritance of economic disadvantage. The children of the poor live in a deprived environment, attend bad schools, are pressed into early school-leaving. In sum, we underinvest in the children of the poor. The issue of the ultimate direction of causation is irrelevant for analysis, although crucial for policy choices. If poverty is the cause of a culture of poverty, an income maintenance policy will eliminate both; if it isn't, it won't.

Functioning of Labor Markets for Low-Wage Workers

It is possible that the problem of low-wage workers is accentuated, though not caused, by imperfect functioning of the labor market. Such imperfect functioning might be reflected in large differentials in unemployment rates, involuntary part-time employment rates, and job vacancy rates by place, industry, occupation, or demographic attributes. It might be partially reflected in labor force participation rates. It might be indicated by differential rates of mobility: geographical, interindustry, occupational, and job mobility. It might be caused by lack of information or by lack of competition, whether taking the form of inflexibility in wage differentials, hiring discrimination, or the balkanization of labor markets resulting from policies of firms, unions, or governments.

Unemployment and Other Labor Market Indicators

The unemployment rate has been the traditional measure of inadequacy of demand for labor. The rate for unskilled and semiskilled workers might be regarded as an indication of the sufficiency or insufficiency of demand for low-wage workers. A low rate does not eliminate all mismatch between skill availabilities and skill demands, but it does eliminate the major mismatches so that remaining structural maladjustments between labor demand and labor supply of low-productivity workers might be reasonably eliminated by modest amounts of training. Unemployment rate differentials by labor market would indicate the need to eliminate the mismatch between location of labor supply and labor demand for low-wage workers.

The industries in which low-wage workers are concentrated may contribute to their unemployment because of seasonality, but cannot account for the large differential in unemployment rate because of their weaker attachment to the labor force. Three other factors also contribute. Unemployment compensation, welfare, and other income supplements present an alternative which is comparable to potential earnings for some low-wage workers, but not for the higher-wage worker. The combination of somewhat unrealistic expectations among some low-skill workers with what Clarence Long has called a "social minimum wage" also reduces their employment. Finally, participation in a subculture of poverty is adverse to employability and also makes the condition of unemployment or nonparticipation, and the receipt of support from sources other than earnings, more acceptable. These reasons for higher unemployment rates among low-wage workers are all compatible with an adequate functioning of the labor market. They suggest an equilibrium unemployment rate (and nonparticipation rate) for low-wage workers substantially higher than for workers in general.

Unemployment rate differentials by occupational group are greater than by major industry group. As expected, they are above average for most low-wage occupational groups, notably nonfarm laborers. Long-term unemployment (twenty-seven weeks and longer) is heavily overrepresented in three occupational groups: operatives, service workers except private household, and nonfarm laborers. Among industries, only construction and agriculture had a high overrepresentation.

The coexistence of high job vacancy rates and high unemployment rates casts doubt on the reliability of unemployment statistics as a measure

TABLE 16
UNEMPLOYMENT RATES
BY OCCUPATION AND INDUSTRY, 1971
(Percent)

Occupation Group		Major Industry Group	
Professional and technical	2.9	Agriculture	7.9
Managers and officials	1.6	Mining	4.1
Clerical	4.8	Construction	10.4
Sales	4.3	Manufacturing, durables	7.0
Craftsmen	4.7	Manufacturing, nondurables	6.5
Operatives	8.3	Transportation and utilities	3.8
Nonfarm laborers	10.8	Trade	6.4
Private household	4.5	Finance, insurance, real estate	3.3
Other service workers	6.6	Service industries	5.6
Farmers and farm laborers	2.6	Government	2.9
Total	5.9	Total	5.9

SOURCE: *Manpower Report of the President,* 1972, pp. 179–180.

of surplus and shortage by occupation and industry. Job vacancy rates have been suggested as indicants of the adequacy of demand, either in isolation or in combination with unemployment rates (the ratio of the two being the indicant in this case). However, there are no statistical series available on job vacancy rates by occupation. (Data for selected manufacturing industries are available since 1969.) Data on help wanted ads and United States Training and Employment Service (USTES) data on positions available are the closest approaches. Conceptual issues must be recognized in compiling a meaningful index of job vacancies as a measure of occupational demand and supply.[66] Vacancies and unemployment are not independent: quits create vacancies and vice versa.

The job vacancy rate in 1966 was higher for semiskilled (operatives) and unskilled (laborers) workers than for the labor force as a whole. It was slightly lower, however, for service workers. In terms of major industry division, services had a higher than average vacancy rate in both March 1965 and March 1966; trade was lower both years; and nondurable manufacturing was lower in 1965 and slightly higher in 1966.[67] If any conclusion can be drawn, it is that vacancy rates cannot explain the large differences in unemployment rates between low-wage and other occupations. The explanation must be found in the high turnover rates which require high vacancy rates in turn for a given level of unemployment, or in the quality of the vacancies.

Hard-to-fill vacancies for unskilled and semiskilled workers were a higher proportion of total vacancies (56 and 58 percent) than for the total economy (50 percent) in April 1965, although unskilled hard-to-fill vacancies were a lower proportion in 1966.[68] By major industry division, however, services had a higher than average rate of hard-to-fill vacancies, although service occupations had a lower than average rate. Pay rates below those prevailing in the area for the occupation account for some of the hard-to-fill vacancies, but do not appear to be a major explanation. A significant difference between low-skill and other occupations, however, is in the duration of vacancies: vacancies lasting three weeks or less are 69.2 percent of the total in service occupations, 54.3 percent for unskilled workers, 55.5 percent for clerical and sales workers, but 25.1 percent for operatives and 24.3 percent for craftsmen.[69]

High unemployment in low-wage occupations may be evidence of excess supply, or of high turnover, or of poor functioning of labor markets. The propensity to change jobs might be expected to be higher for low-wage workers simply because their current jobs are unattractive in terms of pay and in other respects. Some light may be shed by comparing rates of separation, quits, and layoffs in low-wage manufacturing industries. In fact, quit rates by industry show a negative correlation with average hourly earnings of production workers by industry.[70] In 1971, every low-wage two-digit industry had higher quit rates and separation rates than the manufacturing average, and all of them had a higher ratio of quits to separations.

In addition to evidence of excess supply suggested by unemployment rates, there is additional evidence of underemployment. Employees working less than thirty-five hours a week for economic reasons (i.e., involuntarily) were 3.5 percent of whites and 6.4 percent of nonwhites living in urban poverty areas, but only 1.8 and 3.6 percent, respectively, of workers living in nonpoverty areas in 1967.[71]

Evidence of labor force underparticipation cannot be based on comparing rates for low-

TABLE 17
TURNOVER RATES FOR LOW-WAGE
MANUFACTURING INDUSTRIES, 1967
(Per 100 Employees)

Industry	Separations	Quits	Layoffs
Textile products	5.3	3.4	0.9
Apparel	5.7	2.8	2.1
Lumber and wood products	5.3	3.1	1.3
Furniture and fixtures	5.2	3.0	1.1
Rubber and miscellaneous plastic products	4.2	2.1	1.2
Leather and leather products	6.3	3.1	2.1
Miscellaneous manufacturing industries	5.5	2.4	2.1
All manufacturing	4.2	1.8	1.6

SOURCE: *Employment and Earnings Statistics for the United States 1909–1972*, Bureau of Labor Statistics Bulletin no. 1312–9.

productivity workers and other workers since there are differences in health and, among females, there is substantial discretion on labor force participation.

Also useful in gauging underemployment is the labor force response to changes in demand for labor. The elasticity of labor force participation in response to a rise in employment has been estimated at 0.46. (For each additional job created, the labor force increases by 0.46 workers in response.) The elasticity however, is more than four times higher for women (0.9) than for men (0.21). For both sexes it is extremely high for teen-agers (1.8 for males, 2.4 for females).[72] A study of poverty

areas in large cities using 1960 census data found
an elasticity of 3.1 for women in response to a
decline in the unemployment rate. This masked
large differences between the predominantly
white areas (1.5) and the predominantly nonwhite
areas (3.6). The elasticity for all females in the
same metropolitan areas was 1.5, but lower for
white (1.1) than for nonwhite females (1.6).[73]

Job Search and Hiring Efforts

Methods of job search also distinguish many
low-productivity workers from other workers.
Teen-agers, whose attachment in many cases is
casual, also search in a sporadic and casual way.
Considering the range of jobs available for unskilled teen-agers, the expected incremental benefit from additional or more systematic job search
is probably less than the costs, from a private
benefit-cost standpoint. In terms of social costs and
returns, however, additional job search is desirable. Hence, it has been recommended that the
teen-ager's job search be subsidized.[74] A study of
job search by Negroes versus whites in Middle-
town, Connecticut, found that informal methods
predominated in both groups, but that the Negroes
(mainly in low-wage occupations) had less adequate sources of information, both in number and
quality.[75] A study by levels of skill found that the
lower the skill, the smaller the proportion of
workers initiating a job search before leaving their
last job.[76]

Employer hiring costs, the methods and costs

of search by employers, the willingness and ability of both prospective employer and employee to devote resources to matching job openings and workers, are highly related with the level of skill and earnings. A survey of employer hiring channels in Rochester showed a low number and diversity of hiring channels used by firms in recruiting unskilled workers and service workers compared with the channels used in recruiting more skilled workers.[77] A survey of hiring costs in Monroe County, New York, in 1965 and 1966 found sharp differences by occupational group. Manufacturing firms spent an average of $92 per semiskilled and unskilled hire, $150 per clerical worker, but $537 per skilled worker and $1,139 per professional, technical, and managerial hire. For nonmanufacturing firms, the corresponding figures were $94, $130, $103, and $202.[78]

Mobility

High unemployment rates and low wages among low-skill workers could be, in part, the result of low mobility. We have no direct knowledge of mobility. What we have is information on movement. But a lack of movement may be the outcome of a lack of opportunity rather than of an unwillingness to move. (On the other hand, some movement is involuntary; it is the result of job loss.)

Mobility may be considered from several standpoints: (1) geographical; (2) occupational; (3) industrial; and (4) between employers. These are all intercorrelated. It is necessary to distinguish between voluntary and involuntary mobility. The former is presumably optimizing, with moves involving at least an expected improvement. Involuntary mobility, on the other hand, cannot be presumed to improve the worker's position or to be associated with expected improvement. Only the former, therefore, is pertinent in assessing the mobility of the low-productivity worker. Available data often do not distinguish between the two, however. Secondary family workers have no geographical mobility of their own. Their movement is determined by that of the primary wage earner and cannot be assumed to be equilibrating.

Mobility may refer to a propensity, or to actual moves. It is the propensity that measures the tendency of workers to achieve their optimal wage and employment position. Actual moves reflect both potential mobility and the opportunities for improving one's position by a move. If wage rate and unemployment rate differentials are small, there may be fewer moves, but not necessarily less mobility (viewed as a propensity). In fact, with high mobility, differentials inducing moves are rapidly reduced and the number of moves may decline. The fact that wage differentials between regions are greater for low-wage workers suggests that the latter are less mobile than higher-wage workers. The appropriate measure of performance should be a net rather than a gross figure. There is considerable reverse migration back to areas with low wage rate and/or high unemployment rates, suggesting that many migrants do not succeed in

improving their position, and return. There is
evidence that migration is less effective for low-
productivity workers than for other workers.

Low-wage occupations (except farmers and
farm managers) do not have a much lower migration rate than higher-wage occupations (excepting
professional and technical workers). The big difference between occupational groups is in reasons for
migrating. Among the higher-wage occupations,
migration is predominantly to take a job, among
the low-wage ones, to look for a job.[79] One may
infer that the migration process is less efficient and
more costly for the low-wage worker.

The special case of agriculture, whose rapid
decline in employment has involved massive outmigration, has been thoroughly studied. The evidence on the inefficiency of migrating is clear.
Large outmovements are cancelled, to a great
extent, by large return movements. Even though
the age distribution of outmovers and inmovers
differs (inmovers being more common in older age
groups, and outmovers less common), still, net
outmigration from farming is a small proportion—
some 10 percent—of gross outmigration.[80]

Highest rates of occupational mobility are
found among farmers and farm laborers who moon-
lighted. Their rates are four to six times the rates of
those not holding an off-farm job first. This means
that they obtained nonfarm employment in the
same labor market area and before they left
farming. This procedure for increasing the rate and
the efficiency of outflow from farming minimizes
geographical migration, however, and seriously

restricts the number and diversity of employment opportunities off the farm by its geographical constraints.

Nonwhites reveal lower migration rates than whites at all ages; at ages below forty-five, their rate is little more than half that of whites. Furthermore, a much higher proportion of Negroes than of whites migrates to look for a job rather than to take a job they already have. Clearly, most successful migration would be among those who move to take rather than to look for a job. Nevertheless, nonwhite gains from migration are large; between 1950 and 1960, 22 percent of the total growth in nonwhite median income was accounted for by migration, and 20 percent by interoccupational mobility.[81]

Migration rates for women, by occupational group, are substantially lower than for men, except for clerical and kindred workers and service workers (other than private household), where they are slightly higher. The striking differentiation in migration rates, however, is by education: 9.3 percent in 1970 for the male population 25 years and older with not more than eight years of school, 15.8 percent for those with a high school education, and 29.1 percent for those with a college education. There is also a sharp drop in rates with age: 27.5 percent for males aged 20–24, 8.6 percent for males aged 45–64. Finally, the migration rates of family heads with a 1969 family income of less than $3,000 was significantly lower than for other income groups: 13.1 percent versus 16.6 percent for the $3,000–$6,999 class. However, unemployed workers did have a somewhat higher migration rate than employed workers. Only the age-migration rate relation is favorable to low-wage workers. By all other measure, their migration rates compare unfavorably with those of other workers.[82]

Evidence of the willingness of unemployed, predominantly low-wage workers to migrate is provided by experimental labor mobility projects conducted by the Department of Labor in 1965–68.[83] Two-thirds of those offered jobs in different areas accepted. But a check two months after relocation found that 13 percent were unemployed and one-fourth had changed jobs. This suggests that the problem is not just inadequate geographical mobility.

Mazek, using 1960 census data, examined the migration behavior of laborers between metropolitan areas.[84] He regressed migration against the potential unemployment of laborers in 1960 that would have existed had there been no migration of laborers between 1955 and 1960. He found a positive association, which, however, was much stronger for whites than for nonwhites. Thus, migration proved to be equilibrating, reducing unemployment rates for laborers.

Although there is no lack of voluntary job change among low-wage workers, and substantial willingness to migrate in the direction of economic opportunity, there is less evidence of upward occupational mobility and of movements to high-wage industries which would improve their earnings. This is true despite the fact that laborers, service workers, and operatives show high rates of occupational mobility. As in the case of migration, the mechanism of occupational change seems quite inefficient among low-productivity workers. Net upward mobility seems small relative to gross mobility. Studies of mobility between broad occupational groups reveal that: (1) most mobility from low-wage occupations is to other low-wage occupations, with limited improvement, if any, for the mover; (2) there is a mobility barrier separating blue collar and white collar workers. Evidence that the "distance" of occupational moves is small is that there is little relationship between occupational mobility and earnings, but a high correlation with unemployment rates.[85]

Not much upward mobility is to be expected in a short period of time. Over a considerable number of years, however, the changing structure of occupations must reveal considerable upward mobility, as farming and labor occupations decline and professional and technical occupations expand. Blau has studied three relationships over time for men aged 20–64: (1) first occupation by present occupation; (2) father's occupation by first occupation; and (3) father's occupation by present occupation.[86] The resulting matrices reveal that most individuals move only a limited occupational "distance" during their working lives and that the father's occupational level has a strong influence on the occupational level of sons, both in their first and in their current occupation. The matrices also reveal a limited mobility between blue collar and white collar occupational groups.

The intergenerational influence on occupational status and mobility is attested by many studies. Eckland finds that the father's socioeconomic status makes a significant contribution to the son's occupational achievement, independently of its effect on the son's educational career.[87] Rehberg and Wesby have demonstrated the relationship between parental encouragement and educational expectations of high school sophomores and the positive correlation between parental encouragement and the occupational and educational achievement of the father.[88]

Occupational mobility is an inverse function of age. Teen-agers have occupational mixes that are largely transitory; as they acquire experience and additional education, they develop a firmer attachment to the labor force and to career ladders. Experience, it seems, is subject to rapidly decreasing returns, for the occupational mix does not change much after the age of twenty-five.

Agriculture is the biggest net "exporter" of labor. In the past, lumber and wood products and food products have been important seasonal employments for men and women respectively. Construction, besides lacking growth in rural areas, has developed entry restrictions. Textiles and apparel have become important in some areas.[89] All of these offer a shift from farm labor to operative occupations without migration.

"A very high proportion of the occupational mobility out of the farm labor force appears to be in unskilled occupations and into industries where, like agriculture, unskilled labor is rapidly being displaced by machines. Thus, as things seem to be working out, yesterday's unemployed in agriculture may become tomorrow's unemployed factory workers, twice displaced by the substitution of labor by capital."[90]

Wage Differentials

Wage differentials are one way of inducing labor mobility, of bringing about equilibrium in the market for labor. Unresponsiveness of wage differentials places the burden of adjustment on unemployment rate differentials. The evidence on wage differentials is that they respond in equilibrating directions, but that there is a lack of flexibility. One case already noted is that of teenagers, whose high unemployment rate is in some degree attributable to a lack of wage adjustment to the relative growth in the supply of teen-age labor. The persistent differentials between strongly unionized and nonunionized industries is another illustration of inflexibility. Higher wage minima have, on occasion, narrowed differentials in a disequilibrating direction. But disequilibrium is not all caused by employers, unions, and governments. A study of unemployed workers found almost no reduction in their reservation wage—the lowest wage they would accept as a function of the duration of unemployment—even for workers unemployed up to six months.[91]

Keat finds a narrowing of differentials between skilled and unskilled wages, from a ratio of 205 in 1900 to 149 in 1949, to which immigration contributed to an unknown extent.[92] More recently, Segal finds a compression of differentials between skilled and unskilled in major cities during the 1940s, but widening differentials during the 1950s when changes in skill demands favored the more skilled.[93] Cohen finds narrowing skill differentials in blue collar occupations and widening differentials in white collar occupations between 1953 and 1965, a period in which white collar occupations were expanding rapidly.[94] In comparing industry average hourly earnings, Delehanty and Evans have found a widening of the gap between low and high wage manufacturing industries between 1958 and 1963.[95] In their studies there is some consideration of the effect of higher minima in compressing differentials in the South and of the effect of unions in narrowing differentials within and widening them between industries, but there is no serious doubt that differentials are broadly responsive to market forces. These studies are for different time periods and groups of workers. But studies covering the 1950s and later are all compatible with an explanation stressing growth of demand in widening differentials.

On the supply side, the large outflow of labor from farming after World War II widened differentials by increasing the supply of low-skill labor. The rapid increase in the proportion of workers completing high school and, more recently, in the proportion completing college, both tend to narrow differentials by increasing the potential supply of skilled labor. It is difficult to predict the balance of these opposing forces in future years. At higher levels of skill, increased supplies of educated labor will tend to depress skill differentials, and there is no prospect of demand increasing concurrently. At lower levels of skill, supply will tend to fall, and so will demand, but there is some doubt as to which will fall faster. With the extension of federal minimum wages to cover nearly all wage earners, legislation rather than the balance between supply and demand will establish the wage floor for unskilled workers. The tendency has been for increases in the minimum to restore a floor of about half the average hourly earnings of production workers in manufacturing.

Occupational differentials for low-wage occupations are greater in nonmanufacturing than in manufacturing and are usually greatest in retail trade. The generalization is that occupational differentials are least in industries competing regionally and nationally and are greatest in industries, such as retail trade, whose competition is almost exclusively local and whose employees are largely women and secondary family workers.

A critical study of the determinants of wages of unskilled workers took the wages of male janitors as the dependent variable and found the following variables highly correlated with it: (1) the level of wages of skilled workers in the industry; (2) the industry's value of product per worker; and (3) the skill mix (ratio of skilled to total employment).[96] Other studies on occupational wages corroborate this finding that interindustry differentials are more important than interregional differentials.

The differentials between metropolitan and nonmetropolitan wages in low-wage industries and occupations are smaller in the South than in the rest of the nation. Furthermore, skill differentials are greater in the Southern metropolitan areas than in metropolitan areas outside the South. It follows that the South–non-South differentials for low-skill labor are greater than for skilled labor. The indicated equilibrating directions of low-skill labor migration are from the rural South to the urban non-South and from the urban South to the urban non-South.

South–non-South wage differentials by industry consequently are greatest for low-wage industries and are greater between SMSAs than between SMSAs and smaller populated places. In manufacturing, differentials in average wages are greatest, generally, where a small proportion of national employment is in the South. This pattern indicates (a) the leveling influence of previous migration and (b) the potential for future migration of industry to the South. Interregional differences in wages are greater in the industries (retail trade, services) and occupations serving local markets than in those serving regional and national markets.

The South–non-South differentials clearly fit a demand and supply explanation. The fact that differentials are largest for the unskilled and low-skill jobs confirms this judgment. For, migration is highest for the highly skilled, lowest for the least-skilled. Furthermore, it is in the unskilled jobs that the South tends to oversupply the labor market, through a high rate of natural increase, a large agricultural population, and low levels of education and training. These characteristics—of migration, natural increase, farming, and little education —are particularly true of Negroes, for whom the South–non-South wage differentials are much larger than for whites. The preferred hypothesis explaining the larger differentials and the lower wages in the South is an excess supply of low-skill labor as compared with skilled labor. A supplementary assumption is lower geographical mobility of low-skill than of skilled labor.

The discussion has been exclusively in terms of money wages. Insofar as there are interregional differences in cost of living, or metropolitan– nonmetropolitan differences, one would not expect equalization of wage rates even with a perfectly functioning labor market. In fact, there are differences and, therefore, the differentials in real wages are less than indicated by money wages. Not too much should be made of this justification for persisting wage differentials, however. One explanation of wage differentials is a mild climate which keeps the cost of living in the South below that of the non-South. Another, however, is low wages, which also keep down cost of living. But low wages in the South do not explain wage differentials between South and non-South as a labor market equilibrium condition.

The conclusion is that wage differentials reflect labor market conditions and respond to changes in these conditions, despite rigidities introduced by unions, legislation, and worker unwillingness to accept downward wage flexibility. With wages, as with unemployment, we do not know precisely what differentials are called for under equilibrium conditions, and cannot say, therefore, how far actual differentials diverge from equilibrium and what the consequences are in terms of employment, inefficient mobility, and other results.

Conclusions. No single indicant—unemployment, underemployment, labor force participation —is an adequate measure of the precise extent of labor market disequilibrium and of its effect on earnings. Indications of labor surplus include the following: the higher incidence of involuntary part-time work among residents in poverty areas and among nonwhites; the elastic response of labor force participation by women, teen-agers, and nonwhites to increases in employment; the concentration of long-term unemployment among low-wage workers. Some of this disequilibrium results from rigidities that constrain competition, including, in particular, wage rigidities. Some disequilibrium results from frictions that make competition less than perfect: for example, the limited sources of labor market information available to or used by low-wage workers and their inefficient mobility.

Higher unemployment rates for low-wage occupations as well as for females and teen-agers are not conclusive evidence of labor surplus, in view of high vacancy and quit rates. The fact that there are many unfilled openings for low-skill workers does not mean that there is no shortage of jobs for them, only that the problem of job availability is not as important quantitatively as high unemployment and low labor force participation rates would indicate. Nor does the unwillingness of some unskilled workers to accept the jobs that are available suggest that the problem is simply one of attitude. Granted that if all of us were to believe and practice what we preach about the dignity of labor, the employment problem of low-wage, low-skill workers would be greatly ameliorated. But this alone would do nothing to enhance the productivity of the jobs many workers disdain, or the productivity of the workers themselves. On the contrary, were workers less reluctant to take the low-wage, low-skill jobs that are available, upward pressure on their wage rates would be diminished.

Chapter Five
POLICY
ALTERNATIVES

Introduction

Low-wage workers have little in common.
Beyond having low average skill, they are a very
heterogeneous group. They include the very young
and the very old and a high proportion of women
and Negroes.

What is to be done? From the heterogeneity of
low-wage workers it follows that there is not one
but many different problems. For some, nothing
should be done; for most, a wide variety of policies
can be recommended. These policies cannot always be compared as alternatives because, to a
considerable extent, each policy applies to a
different subgroup among low-wage workers and
responds to a different problem.

The alternative policies may be stated universally as: (1) changing the industry mix in order to
reduce radically the share of low-productivity
industries in the economy; (2) changing the occu-

pational mix in order to reduce radically the share of low-skill, low-productivity occupations in the employed labor force; (3) increasing earnings of low-productivity workers in the context of the present industrial and occupational structure; or (4) wage subsidies.

Approaches to eliminating low-productivity industries include unrestricted imports. Such a policy, however, would not affect industries whose markets are local, i.e., retail trade and services. For such industries, the only way to eliminate low-productivity jobs is to change the methods of production radically. In other words, elimination of low-pay jobs requires a major change in the occupational structure of low-productivity industries with local markets.

Approaches to eliminating low-productivity occupations include expanded programs of education, training, information, and relocation as well as the subsidies required to implement all these specific objectives. These measures, however, deal only with the supply side. To cope with the demand side, reducing it for low-level skills and increasing it for the higher-level skills, appropriate changes in industry production techniques would be required. Thus, much change in low-productivity industry and in low-productivity occupations calls for the same type of policy: investment and other initiatives to change the occupational composition of labor requirements in low-productivity industries.

All the policies mentioned above are being acted upon at a fair pace as it is. Should the pace be accelerated? If there are frictions and rigidities hampering the flow of investment in capital and in skills, the adoption of new technology, the change in occupational mix, then the answer is yes. On the other hand, the process may be proceeding at roughly the pace that available technology and market prices justify. To accelerate would require subsidy. Furthermore, to accelerate might aggravate unemployment which would, in part at least, cancel out the gains to low-wage workers.

There remains a policy of directly increasing earnings of low-wage workers without attempting to change occupational or industry mix. Naturally, higher wages will induce substitution of capital for labor and high-skill for low-skill labor; higher wages also will have some effect on the industry and occupation mix through the demand side, unless demand for the products of the industries in question is extraordinarily insensitive to price increases. A wage-raising strategy, therefore, will, in time, induce limited resort to the second strategy, of increasing the skill level of low-productivity workers in order to retain their employability.

Some low-productivity industries will persist, particularly those supplying local markets; some low-productivity occupational slots must remain. For, there are limits to the transformation of production techniques and of the composition of demand in response to higher wages for low-skill individuals. There are limits to the flexibility of labor, particularly in the short run. Not all individuals are able, or willing, to absorb substantial amounts of training. In the short run, where occupational change must be accompanied by significant geographical and/or industry mobility, many are not prepared to make the necessary adjustments. Since there are frictions and constraints in all directions, it seems necessary to pursue a multiple strategy in order to maximize desired effects and/or minimize the costs of achieving them.

It is possible to raise incomes of low-productivity workers through wage subsidies, family allowances, and income maintenance programs of various sorts without directly increasing labor costs to the employer. How these transfers are financed, and their cost and revenue implications for the producer, is a separate issue. However, such policies are responsive to the problems of poverty and low income, not to the problems of low productivity or even low earnings, as such. If such policies lead to substitution of some low-productivity workers for other (perhaps low-productivity) workers, again, the needs for the other policy alternatives mentioned earlier are affected.

The wage objective must be made clear. One possible objective is to reduce relative wage differentials—to compress the wage structure. Another is to attain a given absolute real wage. In the latter case, relative differentials may be reduced until the target absolute level is attained, but need not be influenced thereafter. If the objective is nonspecific, only to raise the wages of the lowest x percent of the labor force, then it can never be achieved short of absolute equality because otherwise there will always be a lowest x percent.

If the end is to increase national output or develop individual potentials, then such a goal is not expressible in terms of relative wages or in terms of a given absolute real wage. The most effective measures for increasing national and individual productivity are implemented first, whether they apply to low-wage workers or to higher-wage workers. The latter may indeed benefit more than the former from training—and contribute more as the result of it.

Only if the ultimate objective is the alleviation of poverty can it be expressed, however approximately, in terms of wage differentials or wage levels. The definition of poverty is beyond our scope. If it is a given real income level, then with economic progress the problem of low-wage workers will disappear. If poverty is defined in relative terms, it is insoluble. In our day, a choice of definitions is not yet critical. For absolute, not just relative, poverty is still with us.

With economic progress in the context of a free market, the real wages of low-productivity workers will continue to rise. But there is no reason to expect that the relative wage differential (much less the absolute wage differential) between low-productivity workers and the average worker will be greatly diminished either through the normal operations of the market or through public policies (e.g., training, mobility assistance, regional development) which work through the market. The only sure way to reduce permanently and significantly the relative differential is through permanent transfer programs—through political decisions overruling the distribution occurring through a free market for products and factors of production, including labor.

Wage Policies

Raising the Fair Labor Standards Act Minimum Wage

The simplistic approach toward raising wages of low-productivity workers is minimum wage legislation. The present minimum is not high enough to satisfy our distributional objectives among workers, or for the population, insofar as distributional objectives can be achieved through the labor market. The head of a family of four can work full time all year and still fall below the poverty line. A substantial increase in the Fair Labor Standards minimum would be required to affect directly and significantly most workers classified as low-wage. An increased minimum would be a direct response only to the welfare objective, not to the productivity objective. A policy successful in raising real wages of low-wage workers implies redistribution achieved by compressing the wage structure or by shifting income from nonlabor sources. Such a policy assumes that wage increases will not be dissipated by price increases and will not reduce employment of low-wage workers. If these extreme assumptions are relaxed, then every policy must weigh positive and negative effects, both on welfare and on output.

Employer responses to higher wages of low-productivity workers may include upgrading their skill and raising their productivity so that positive output effects will counteract the negative output effects of disemployment. To the extent that higher skills are substituted for lower skills, however, some of the substitution will not be upgrading workers, but will be the hiring of more skilled workers, thus worsening the welfare effects on low-wage, low-skill workers who are discharged instead of being upgraded.

Any increase in the legal minimum will raise earnings of some low-wage workers and disemploy others. The fear that the first effect might be cancelled by the second has kept increases in the minimum wage within bounds. The largest in point of impact was the $1.60 minimum effective in February 1968, at which time 17 percent of covered employees were earning less than this amount (some of them to be raised by stages to the general minimum). The cost of raising them all to the new minimum, however, was still only 1.1 percent of payroll, and the average wage increase required to comply with the law was sixteen cents an hour for subminimum-wage employees.[1]

The constraints on a policy of raising the legal wage floor are the side effects: adverse employment effects on low-wage areas caused by eliminating interregional wage differentials in low-wage industries; adverse employment, and possibly payroll, effects on low-wage industries; and adverse employment and income effects on low-productivity workers directly, as well as indirectly, through their concentration in low-wage areas and industries.

Federal minimum wage coverage, although greatly extended during the past decade, is still far from complete. The self-employed, unpaid family workers and employees in very small trade and service establishments are excluded or exempted. State and local minimum wage laws extend coverage in some cases but not in others. Earnings in some uncovered activities may be adversely affected by the disemployment effects of higher minimum wages on the supply of job seekers. This is as much an argument for more universal coverage as for restraint in raising the statutory minimum wage.

Adverse employment effects may result from price increases leading to reduced sales or a shift of demand to imports, or they may result from the employer's adjustments to higher wages for low-productivity workers, which may include substituting machinery, higher-skill workers, or other methods reducing the demand for low-skill workers. The likelihood and extent of these adverse effects varies widely by industry. Some low-wage industries can raise wages for low-skill workers with smaller repercussions on unit costs and prices or sales than others. Specifically, local market industries and public employment offer greater latitude for such a policy than industries selling in a commercial market in competition over extensive areas. The former are sheltered from competition with other areas not subject to the same minimum, or less affected by it.

The magnitude of effect also varies by region. This is the reason Puerto Rico was given an exemption from the Fair Labor Standards Act minimum following economically disastrous attempts to apply it. Although wage differentials have been sharply reduced in most industries, wages in Puerto Rico are still sufficiently below levels in the South to cause severe adjustment problems for many industries. Unfortunately, it is the lowest-wage regions and the lowest-wage workers that are most likely to suffer the adverse side effects of a higher minimum wage.

From a longer-range standpoint, higher minimum wages reduce the rate at which new low-wage jobs are created and preclude creation of jobs whose productivity is below the minimum wage in covered employments. To the extent such an outcome reduces employment, it aggravates the poverty problem for some and may also reduce the growth of national output. In brief, productivity of the individual worker, national output, and reduction of poverty are mutually compatible only on the assumption that unemployment does not rise. The evidence is fairly conclusive, however, that it does rise.

It is often claimed that low-wage labor is unlike any other service in that an increase in its price does not reduce the amount demanded. The reasoning is that direct reductions in employment are counteracted by indirect increases. These increases result from the fact that some low-wage workers receive increases in pay, and the assumption is that in spite of some direct reduction in

employment, there is an increase in total payroll of
low-wage workers. The increase in payroll is spent
and generates an employment multiplier effect. No
serious study has ever demonstrated, however, that
a higher minimum wage has increased total payrolls of low-wage workers. Hence, this indirect
purchasing power employment-generating effect is
likely to have a negative sign. Even if there were a
positive payroll effect, it is stretching the imagina-
tion to expect any large portion of the resulting
jobs created to be among low-wage, or formerly
low-wage, workers.

Higher Wages in Local Market Industries

It may appear that wages of low-productivity
workers can be raised with impunity in industries
that do not compete nationally. Except for the
effects of a price-sensitive product demand on the
demand for labor, costs can be raised within wide
limits. However, such a policy may also indirectly
raise the costs of low-wage export industries,
weakening the economic base of the entire community. Among industries employing significant
numbers of low-pay workers are hotels and motels,
eating and drinking places, retail stores, hospitals
and nursing homes, and laundries and cleaning
establishments. Hotels and motels have little effect
on local costs because residents make little use of
them. They are an export industry whose position
is not highly competitive unless they are resort
facilities. Otherwise, they are used by individuals
who visit the city for reasons other than to stay in

them. Hospitals and nursing homes are of large and growing importance as local costs. But to the extent that expenses are largely covered by medical insurance, medicare, medicaid, etc., increases in local costs do not affect the competitive position of the local community. Only to the extent that the expenses are borne directly by households and business in the area do they affect comparative local costs of living and doing business. Since from the viewpoint of any one family they are infrequently used, and since the greatest use is by individuals not in the labor force, high local medical and hospital labor costs are not likely significantly to affect wage costs or the competitive position of exporting industries. Restaurants and other eating and drinking establishments, and laundry and cleaning establishments, are mainly used by local residents, and higher labor costs can raise local costs of living and wages in export industries. Their use can be largely avoided, however. This is not true of retail stores, which, however, have a low ratio of payroll to sales, a national average of 11 percent.

These industries, plus agriculture, are the main ones affected by the extensions of coverage of the Fair Labor Standards Act during the 1960s. Their lack of union organization deprives them of any other effective agency for wage increases in the absence of a labor shortage.

Adverse effects of raising wages in local market industries result from interarea differences in such wages; they affect the competitive position of export activities in areas with higher local

market industry wages, and they affect the choice
of location for new investment (or expansion) in
such activities. The role of local market industries,
and therefore the scope for wage increases in
them, has grown significantly. First, with higher
incomes, a larger proportion of income is spent on
local services and retail trade. Second, with a
slower than average growth in productivity in trade
and services, a higher proportion of employment is
to be found in these predominantly local market
activities. Third, with urbanization and metropoli-
tanization, a higher proportion of economic activity
has become local market oriented. As a rough
estimate, 60 percent of employment in cities of one
million population or more (more than one-third of
the nation) is local-market. By the same token, the
argument that raising wages of low-productivity
workers in this or that trade or service industry has
no appreciable effect on the viability of export
industry breaks down when a wage-raising policy
applies to all trade and service and other local
market activities.

Higher Wages in Public Services

The wages of labor in competitive markets for
its products are determined by the market prices of
its products and by labor productivity. Actual
wages are only an approximation to this theoretical
norm. There are divergences from, and imperfec-
tions of, competition which make the wages of
some labor lower, and of some labor higher, than
the value of its marginal product. The latter wage

structure, of course, cannot persist for long, since labor costing more than the value of its product will not continue to be employed for long. Another source of divergence from the norm is the fact that in an establishment there may be many different kinds of labor, working with a diversity of equipment, producing a multiplicity of products. Although the total income of the factors of production may be readily imputed from the value added in production (at market prices), the imputation of this aggregate income among the component skills, occupations, and individuals is arbitrary. It is not possible to vary a single skill and, in this way, determine its contribution to total output. Several skills may be essential; without them, there can be no output; but the total income cannot be imputed more than once. Still, competitive wages for particular skills develop in a well-organized market for labor. In some of its employments it is possible to establish roughly how much a given sort of labor is worth, and this sets an upper limit to its wage.

For many goods and services there is no competitive market. They are produced for (and possibly by) a single customer: the federal government. Or they are produced for many governments, but the market areas of the goods or services (drinking water, fire protection) are so small that each producer is, or faces, a single buyer. In such cases, the upper limit to wages is derived from the maximum price the local government is willing to pay for a service; the lower limit is derived from the opportunity wage of the labor—how much it could obtain in its next best alternative employment. Often there is a wide difference between upper and lower limits, and, therefore, the possibility of considerable indeterminacy in the price of labor. This is true, for instance, of firemen, policemen, judges, garbage collectors, and teachers. In some cases, such as teachers, the cost of labor is the principal item, and the product—primary and secondary education—is directly evaluated by local governments, if not by electorates; salaries are largely determined by public willingness to pay. In other cases, there are joint products and important joint inputs, so that considerable indeterminacy exists about imputation within the larger limits for the total product set by the government or the electorate. Some of the dirty, low-skill jobs in public health facilities are in this category.

Where market measures of labor productivity are ambiguous or do not exist, there are two alternative ways of defining low-productivity labor: (1) the opportunity wage which the labor in question would be able to earn in its next best alternative employment; and (2) the qualifications required for the job. A trash collector may be better paid than an elementary school teacher, but his market-determined wage in alternative employments is lower, and the qualifications required for the job are also much less selective. Thus, he is properly defined as a low-productivity worker and the secondary school teacher as a much higher productivity worker, even though the wage in neither case is derived from a product priced in a competitive market.

The constraint on wage increases as the pre-

ferred solution to low earnings in the public sector
is not the availability of substitute products which
precludes or limits wage increases in the market.
Two other consequences also must be considered
in a wage escalation strategy in the private sector:
input substitutability, which may replace low-
productivity labor either with machinery or with
higher-productivity labor, and price-sensitivity
(elasticity) of demand for the product. In fact, there
is substitutability on the product side, at least
technically, for most government services (schools
and trash collection can be supplied by the
market), but to the extent that they are not financed
by user charges, the substitutability approaches
zero, for the incremental cost of public services to
the user approaches zero. As a result, the effective
demand for most public services is less cost-
sensitive than for similar private services. The
question is what is the political elasticity of
demand for public education or police protection,
for example, as a function of their costs. In public
education, the supply of pupils through age 15 (or
older, in some states) is assured by law. The
response to price is in terms of quality rather than
quantity and in terms of education and training for
individuals 16 and over, who are not required by
law to be in school full time. In most other
activities, there is substantial discretion as to both
quantity and quality.

This discretion sets limits on what increases in
wages are allowable in terms of the resulting
reduction in the number of jobs, even if quantity is
relatively fixed. Where, as in hospitals, there are

close private competitors, the quantity of public hospital services could be highly variable, and a shift to private hospitals might be a feasible response to excessive wage increases.

Data on trends in state and local government suggest that demand for public services is income-elastic.[2] More pertinent is the price elasticity of demand for public services employing numerous low-wage workers. Presumably, price elasticity is low to the extent the public is unaware of unit cost increases in particular services, or it influences expenditures mainly in the aggregate only, through its response to taxation. Studies of local government responses to federal matching grants bear indirectly insofar as they simulate response elasticity over the price reductions to the local government implicit in various federal matching grant ratios. The findings are not conclusive, but suggest elastic response.[3] What we would need to know, however, is the response to a unit cost increase that is simulated by a reduction in the federal matching ratio.

The limits to a policy of raising wages of low-productivity workers in public employment (and/or of expanded public employment of such workers) are set by the willingness of local electorates to finance the costs and by the responses of business to the higher costs of local government. At the city and county level, this means primarily the sensitivity of business to differentials in property tax rates. With few exceptions, this sensitivity seems to be low; differences in land costs may prove a much bigger item in determining property tax liability, which itself may not be significant in costs or even in differential costs of alternative locations. For local governments near state boundaries, sales taxes are the most sensitive to tax rate differentials because of the possibility of shifting place of purchases without change of residence or employment.

Perhaps of greater importance than the overstressed effect of tax rate differentials[4] is the possible sacrifice of other government services in quality or quantity, a sacrifice that would adversely affect local amenities and the costs of doing business. Because of the association of tax costs with the level of government services, studies on the effects of tax rate differentials on economic growth do not support the hypothesis that the higher tax areas are adversely affected. But the proposed policies do not involve the association of high tax rates with high levels of government services, only with high levels of transfer payments to low-productivity workers in the guise of higher wages to such workers in public employment. Since local government jurisdictions with the highest concentration of such workers tend to be low-income and low tax-base, such transfers are likely to affect the quality of the local public infrastructure and amenities unless financed by higher-level governments.

Lower Minimum Wage Rates for Teen-agers

The complexity of the problems of low-wage workers is such that, ironically, some proposals to alleviate the problems recommend raising the minimum wage while other proposals recommend lowering it.

It has been proposed that the unemployment problem of teen-agers can be reduced by permitting them to work for less than the federal minimum wage. This would not increase earnings of those employed, but would increase the number earning. More important than the net effect on teen-age payrolls would be the opportunity provided to acquire experience, training, and skills which would, in time, lift many from low-wage employment—an opportunity denied to many teen-agers who cannot get jobs. One qualification is a probably unenforceable "antipirating" clause: that any increase in jobs for teen-agers be not just a transfer of employment from older, and also low-wage, workers to younger workers.

The assumption behind this proposal is that there is an inadequate number of jobs available for teen-agers at the standard minimum. Teen-agers are high-cost employees because of lack of experience, high turnover rates, etc. Therefore, many are not hired as long as employers must pay essentially the same wage to teen-agers as to older workers.

As we have seen, most of the teen-age unemployment rate is the result of entry and reentry. Even so, more jobs could reduce the average duration of unemployment for entrants and reentrants, and, therefore, the average rate for teen-agers. But average duration is already low. What net increase in job openings might result from a lower minimum wage is not known. The beneficial effect would depend on the supply response to lower wage rates. Even at the standard minimum, many unemployed youth turn down work. Others (some of whom are not in school) are not in the labor force because they do not find available openings attractive. One consequence of lower wage rates would be reduced labor force participation; another might be higher turnover and possibly higher unemployment rates. There are other teen-agers, of course, who would be willing to work at jobs paying less than the current minimum who would be hired if the wage were lowered. At this time, there is no quantitative estimate of the net outcome, but it looks less promising as alternatives to earned income improve.[5] Amendments to the Fair Labor Standards Act permit payment of wages 15 percent below the minimum for learners and student workers, but very little use has been made of these exemptions.

An alternative eliminating some drawbacks of a lower minimum wage for teen-agers would be a wage subsidy paid to the employer.[6] The teen-ager would receive the standard wage. This approach would not discourage labor force participation by teen-agers, since none would get a lower wage. It would encourage job creation for teen-agers, since employers would pay a lower wage net of subsidy. The possibility of transferring jobs from older workers to teen-agers would remain, but the duration of this effect would be strictly limited. This policy could be costly since it would involve a subsidy payment to employers of teen-agers who are already employed (who are nearly 90 percent

of all teen-agers in the labor force). The cost could
be reduced by limiting subsidies to certain classes
of teen-agers, such as high school dropouts, with
highly unfavorable unemployment experience. But
one may question the desirability of encouraging
more persons to drop out of high school by
improving job and earnings prospects in this way,
or one may question whether it is desirable to
place other teen-agers at a disadvantage in the
labor market.

One of the factors in the high rate of teen-age
unemployment has been the large increase in the
number of teen-agers, a result of the high birthrates in the late 1940s and 1950s. Teen-agers have
been an increasing proportion of the labor force
despite higher rates of school attendance. This
trend is now reversing. The 16–19 age group is
increasing slowly and will actually decline in the
1980s. Whatever net benefits might be expected
from a lower minimum wage for teen-agers, they
are likely to be less in the future than they would
have been in the past decade.

To the extent that high unemployment among
low-skill workers is not a voluntary response to
available jobs and wages, but a consequence of a
lack of jobs with minimal skill requirements, even
in a full-employment economy, the question is
why there is a lack of such jobs. One answer is that
the value-productivity of the unemployed is less
than the minimum wage. It is difficult to think of
additional reasons, other than the lack of information or discrimination in the market for low-skill
labor. Adverse effects on unemployment of adults,
in particular nonwhites and women, have also

been observed as a consequence of raising the minimum. Some economists, therefore, have advo-cated a policy of slowing or stopping increases in the minimum wage for all, not just for teen-agers, allowing the ratio of the minimum to the average wage to fall.

In sum, minimum wage policy has little to contribute. Increases sufficient to narrow differen-tials significantly between low-productivity and other workers would have serious side effects on employment. Not much should be expected from a lower minimum wage for teen-agers, but its effects on employment may be worth testing on an experimental basis. Somewhat more can be gained from selective wage increases in local market industries and particularly in public employment. Limits are set by the indirect effects of higher local costs on the competitive position of the community and by the labor-saving reactions of local em-ployers. Wage subsidies provide incentives to employ low-productivity labor, but may result largely in substitution of some employees for others. Gains from wage-raising policies directly are the result of redistribution alone.

Policies Affecting Demand for Low-Skill Workers

Whereas the level of wages in the economy is determined by productivity, the differentials by skill, industry, place, and occupation are predomi-nantly determined by demand and supply condi-tions. Thus, there are three routes to raising wages of low-productivity workers: increasing the av-

erage productivity of the economy; reducing the
supply of low-productivity workers, or its rate of
increase; and increasing the demand for low-
productivity workers.

Increasing national productivity is a goal explicitly recognized in the Full Employment Act of
1946 whose intentions, however, are much broader
than just improving the wages of low-wage
workers.

Increasing demand for low-skill workers runs
counter to long-term trends in this and other
economies. What can be considered are policies
that would increase such demand temporarily, or
which would slow down decreases in demand.
They involve reducing employment costs to the
firm, through wage subsidies, better information,
and reduced risks; diverting demand from imports
to domestic production; increase in public employment; reduction of geographic imbalances through
regional development of areas with surpluses of
low-skill labor.

Policies on the demand side should not ignore
what happens on the supply side. While increasing
demand for low-skill labor, supply policies increase the supply of higher skills and reduce that
of low-skill workers. If each set of policies ignores
the other set, the solution to one problem could
generate another problem of its own.

Improving the Trade Balance

Low-wage labor employed in industries with
extensive markets which have the possibility of

exports or face competition from imports, or both, can be affected by foreign trade policies, specifically tariffs and quotas. Protection from imports can allow such industries to raise wage rates with relative impunity. In effect, protection reduces the price elasticity of demand for their products over a price range up to the point where the tariff ceases to keep out imports. In the case of quotas, price elasticity is reduced at all prices. Naturally, the benefit to domestic workers depends on how elastic the U.S. demand is if imports are ruled out on the supply side.

The question is, first, to what extent are low-wage workers already being protected by import restrictions; how much worse would they fare, in terms of wages and/or employment, were foreign trade free? Second, what is the scope for increasing tariffs, establishing quotas, and reducing the size of quotas in order to raise the wages and/or employment of low-wage workers?

Several attempts have been made to measure the "effective tariff," that is, the amount of protection afforded an industry and its labor force by a tariff rate which applies to a product, much of whose value may have been added in supplying industries. Effective tariff is the tariff applied to the value added by the last stage processing industry. The effective rate of protection of labor in low-wage industries examined is indicated in Table 18.(In the simplest case, it is the tariff rate divided by labor cost as a percentage of product price.)

It is clear that many low-wage manufacturing industries and much agricultural employment are

TABLE 18
PROTECTION OF LABOR BY DETAILED
INDUSTRY
(Percent)

SIC	Industry title	Effective labor rates of protection*	
2031	Canned and cured seafoods	64.6	91.5
2033	Canned fruits and vegetables	409.2	597.6
2121	Cigars	100.4†	101.5†
2141	Tobacco stemming and redrying	307.2	357.6
2251	Full-fashioned hosiery mills	171.1	171.0
2256	Knit fabric mills	662.5	—
2272	Tufted carpets and rugs	195.4	330.4
2295	Coated fabrics not rubberized	26.8	35.4
2311	Men's and boys' suits and coats	44.7	47.0
2341	Women's and children's underwear	215.6	293.0
2385	Waterproof outergarments	59.9	70.9
2511	Wood furniture, not upholstered	39.6	47.0
2643	Bags, except textile bags	109.4	125.9
3079	Plastic products, n.e.c.	44.1	55.8
3151	Leather gloves	195.2	213.9
3871	Watches and clocks	143.1†	175.3†

SOURCE: Giorgio Basevi, "The U.S. Tariff Structure: Estimates of Effective Rates of Protection of U.S. Industry and Industrial Labor," *Review of Economics and Statistics*, May 1966, table 4. Data are based on the 1958 Census of Manufacturers and on 1958–60 tariff data.

* Column three assumes that the tariff on inputs other than labor is 5.1 percent; Column four assumes it to be 1 percent.
†Total rates of protection rather than labor-rates.

heavily protected already. By implication, free imports would have serious adverse effects on low-wage labor in these industries. Low-wage industries that receive substantial protection through informal quotas are textiles and apparel, both of which also receive substantial protection through tariffs. The ability of the United States to raise tariffs and to establish quotas is narrowly constrained by the General Agreement on Tariffs and Trade, as well as by prospects of retaliation.

Considering trade policy only from the narrow standpoint of low-wage workers, it appears there is limited prospect for raising wages and/or employment by greater protection. Export subsidies for industries that require protection from imports to maintain wage rates and/or employment would be an exorbitant way of assisting low-productivity workers. Foreign trade policies cannot affect most low-productivity workers in trade and services, nor many in manufacturing, because their industry does not compete internationally.

There are other ways to improve the trade balance, such as dollar devaluation and reduction in foreign barriers to U. S. exports. It is the announced policy of the federal government to reduce the trade deficit, but for reasons largely unconnected with concern for low-wage workers in trade and services or in manufacturing. Even improving the balance by the $10 billion proposed by former Secretary of Treasury Connally would have no direct effect on most low-wage workers. It makes a difference, however, whether the improvement in trade balance results from an expansion of exports or a contraction of imports. Since United States export industries are higher-wage, higher-skill than domestic industries facing import competition, more is to be gained directly by reducing imports than by expanding exports. Indirectly, the reverse could be true. Since improving the trade balance through export expansion is more conducive to economic growth, it would raise employment and earnings of low-wage workers.

Subsidies to Employers of Low-Productivity Workers

To the extent that the high unemployment rates of low-skill workers are the consequence of low wages (high quit rates, withholding of labor), then job creation is not a relevant policy. Better jobs, or higher pay, would be necessary. But if the market for low-skill labor is highly competitive, as it appears to be, higher wages may require subsidies. Subsidies may take two forms, both of which have been suggested. The first is wage subsidies to employers. The second is public service employment or government as employer of last resort.

The issues in connection with wage subsidies center around which employers would get subsidies, for what employees, and under what conditions. One approach to bounding the policy has been the suggestion that subsidies be given to employers in central city ghettos, in behalf of residents of those areas. Other approaches would not limit employers to any particular location, but would limit subsidies to particular classes of

employees. Already mentioned is the suggestion
that subsidies be paid in behalf of teen-agers. Two
other feasible classifications would be by level of
education: high school dropouts only, and by race:
Negroes only.

Two basic forms of subsidies have been recommended: tax credits and outright payments. The
case for tax credits is the assurance that the firms
benefiting from them are economically sound, and
that, therefore, the jobs they provide have longer-
term security. The case against them is that tax
credits eliminate tax-exempt employers from participation, including state and local governments
and nonprofit organizations. The case for grants,
apart from their wider potential coverage, is their
flexibility, as well as the more explicit accounting
of program costs.[7]

Several criteria have been suggested for determining the amount and duration of subsidy. Most
commonly, proposals for subsidy are geared to the
costs, or excess costs, of hiring and training the
disadvantaged, implying a subsidy of rather short
duration. To the extent that training costs cannot
be separated from production costs, grants or tax
credits become, in effect, lump sum payments for
hiring the selected group of disadvantaged
workers. To the extent that the expectation of
increased productivity through work and associated training experience is not realized, or not
realized to the extent of making the individual
employable at standard wages, then the subsidy
must continue indefinitely. This possibility, however, has not been suggested for the private sector.

A final criterion for determining the amount of subsidy has been suggested by Thurow. He criticizes the focus on inputs, i.e., training, because there is little incentive to economize on training costs and because the objective is higher earnings, for which training may not be the only approach, nor even a necessary one for many disadvantaged workers. The incentives needed are for raising the incomes of the disadvantaged, and, hence, subsidies should be geared to pay increases over a five-year period.

The difficulties with all these proposals are of a practical nature. How can the government avoid compensating employers for doing what they might have done anyway? There is evidence from the operation of the National Alliance of Businessmen JOBS program that many of those hired and trained are not perceptibly different from those the firms are already hiring.[8] Conversely, there are fears that employment is simply transferred from other workers to selected impact groups. This fear is based on an assumption of an inadequate number of jobs. At the very least, the jobs and employment prospects of other low-productivity workers who are employable, and employed, without public subsidy are adversely affected. Unless the calibration of payments to provide inducement to employ normally unemployable workers can avoid adverse impacts on employable low-productivity workers, this policy cannot be recommended.

Buchanan and Moes have suggested payroll subsidies to employers in labor surplus areas, financed by a state tax on wages, in order to reduce forced migration of labor for lack of employment opportunities.[9] Their suggestion introduces not wage flexibility, but flexibility in labor costs to the employer and a reduced disposable income for workers, although not reduced wages. The objective is to increase employment. State and local subsidies for industry in the form of tax exemptions, free land, shell buildings, and contributed services have been common, although they have not been financed by a tax on wages. They are not aimed solely at jobs for the unemployed or for low-wage workers. The basic objection to all these policies is that they induce an inefficient geographical distribution of economic activity, reducing national productivity.[10]

The federal government already has policies favoring employers of low-wage workers indirectly: a procurement policy favoring contractors in depressed areas, and exemption from federal taxes of employers in Puerto Rico (many of whom are exempted from Commonwealth of Puerto Rico taxes as well). The program directly aimed at employment for the hard-core unemployed is the above-mentioned NAB–JOBS program which involves payment by the federal government to employers to cover the excess costs of hiring and training and retaining disadvantaged workers. The target groups are, first, members of minorities, with practical emphasis on Negroes; second, workers less than twenty-two years old or aged forty-five and older; third, high school dropouts; and fourth, handicapped workers.

The Government as Employer of Last Resort

The government as an employer of last resort is a relatively new recommendation, although the practice goes back for centuries. Our nation's large-scale experience with the approach harks back to the 1930s, a time of mass unemployment. The new proposal, however, is applicable under conditions of high employment.[11] It is not a policy for raising wages of low-skill workers, but of assuring them jobs and income. As an alternative to subsidies to employers, it avoids the need to certify eligible workers or employers.

The issues are (1) what should the wage be, and (2) what should workers hired under this approach do? Since its objective is to provide employment, not to raise wages, the wages paid should not be higher than the federal minimum wage. (Still, the wages of millions who are not covered by the federal minimum and who are earning less than the minimum would be raised.) In effect, such a policy would establish a universal federal minimum wage. It also would counteract the disemployment caused by a minimum wage which is higher than the value productivity of some workers. The work to be done has conflicting objectives: utility and lack of competition with work done or potentially performed by business. The difficulty of achieving these objectives is increased insofar as work would have to be provided in every community where there are long-term unemployed. New job creation and job restructuring are essential complements.

Such a program might have several adverse side effects. The one most feared is the program's effect on work attitudes and behavior of those employed at wages little better than those paid by such a program and on the work incentives of low-skill, low-wage workers. A substantial wage differential might be required in the private sector to provide incentives for employment and for work discipline. Such a differential, in turn, would affect production methods and occupational hiring requirements. Governments, on the other hand, might find it impossible to maintain performance standards, which may be incompatible with an unqualified job guarantee. Public service employment might degenerate into a camouflaged guaranteed income. Public service employment has one advantage over wage subsidies to private employers of hard-to-employ workers. It minimizes competition for work with other employees. Public service employment programs seek to increase the demand for selected groups of workers by subsidizing the performance of tasks not previously performed, or performed on a lesser scale. The work performed would not have been done otherwise because the state and local governments involved were unwilling or unable to pay the full cost of its performance.

The federal government is already engaged in the role of employer of last resort on a modest scale and in various guises.[12] Grants to state and local welfare agencies for Work Experience and Training (WET) projects give priority to unemployed parents and other adults. The Neighbor-

hood Youth Corps finances employment sponsored
by public agencies and private nonprofit organizations. The New Careers Program places enrollees
in subprofessional jobs in private organizations.
The Job Corps provides residential work–training
centers for disadvantaged youth. Operation Main-
stream, on the other hand, provides public employment in conservation work for the aged and for
disadvantaged people in rural areas. Most of these
programs (excepting the last) stress their training
component and, by implication, their short-term
nature from the viewpoint of the participant.
Public employment need have no such implication.

The Work Incentive Program (WIN), established by the 1967 amendments to the Social
Security Act, includes among its components the
placement of welfare enrollees in public service
jobs if they cannot be placed in regular jobs or
benefit substantially from training. The public
service jobs include employment in private nonprofit organizations as well as in all levels of
government, with the employer paying at least 20
percent of the enrollee's wages. The program
remained minuscule until 1971 when the Emer-
gency Employment Act greatly expanded funding
and geared it to national and local unemployment
rates. By late 1972, public service employment was
providing some 180,000 jobs.

All of these efforts combined fall far short of
converting the government into employer of last
resort. Limited funds have precluded public service employment of more than a small proportion

of hard-to-employ low-wage workers. In any case,
the government as employer of last resort will not
eliminate the problem of low-skill workers who
choose to remain unemployed, or not in the labor
force, rather than accept humble jobs at low pay.

Shifting the Risks of Employing Low-Productivity Workers

In any cooperative work effort, a worker's
irresponsibility may impose losses on the employer greater than the worker's contribution to the
value of product. There are moral hazards in any
job. Bank presidents have been known to betray
their trust. As an extreme example, the unskilled
job of night watchman involves both preventing
theft and an opportunity to pilfer. If an applicant
has several convictions for robbery, the employer
would only hire the applicant at a negative wage.
Skill, education, and experience have nothing to
do with it.

Only policies which will shift the risk of loss
from the employer can hope to increase employment of individuals presumed to be high risks—
many of whom are not low-productivity. Bonding
is an established means of avoiding, at a price, the
loss which may be attributed to the behavior of a
specific employee. But some of the less employable low-productivity workers are not commer-
cially bondable.

There are other hazards, not moral, but involving carelessness or lack of skill and resulting
in damages to equipment, supplies, or harm to

fellow employees. This type of risk is associated with lack of skill and experience and is reducible through training.

Not all the exceptional risks and uncertainties facing the employer of low-productivity workers are associated with his employees. Some of them are environmental. The employer located in the central city ghetto faces, or may feel that he faces, additional risks due to his location. Insurance companies may concur by charging him higher premiums than he would have to pay at another location, or by refusing to insure him at all. If such a location is considered desirable in order to improve employment and earnings of low-wage workers, then the employer must be able to shift the excess uncertainty, or the excess cost, as the case may be.

Private insurers will impose on the employer the additional costs of verifying covered losses. Not all the excess costs and risks of employing low-productivity workers are easily quantified. The government could avoid them by a subsidy covering estimated risks supplementary to any compensation for the higher hiring and training costs or for lower productivity.

For high-risk employees, whether or not they are low-wage or low-productivity, the competitive wage model, claiming that with downward wage flexibility it is possible to employ everyone, could imply zero or negative wages. Most high-risk employees' contribution to output is smaller than their potential for harm.

A public policy of absorbing the excess costs of

employing high-risk workers does not create jobs; it risks transferring demand from other workers. Subsidy of employment in central cities is a policy properly evaluated in terms of urban structure and functioning, not in terms of low-wage workers alone. A policy running against the trends, if not the logic, of urban development is unlikely to show up well on a cost-effectiveness basis relative to alternative policies.

Nonwage Employment Costs

Wage supplements may be classified into those, such as pension plans, whose cost is long deferred from the viewpoint of the employer of any specific workers and those, such as medical insurance, whose costs, although a function of the age of the employee, basically are not deferred costs. Since the typical employer is not a self-insurer, but purchases insurance for his employees, there are current costs to be paid by him and by the employee, to the extent that the insurance or pension is contributory.

To the extent that rights to pensions, medical care, compensation, etc., are proportional to earnings, presumably the employment prospects of low-wage individuals are unaffected. Most company pension plans are proportional to earnings. On the other hand, other types of nonwage labor costs such as health and medical insurance are not related to the individual's earnings.

Insofar as the employer bears a substantial part of the nonwage costs of employment which are

unrelated to earnings rates (or to length of employment) he has an incentive to minimize his turnover
by retaining workers in slack periods and working
overtime in boom periods, rather than hiring and
discharging in keeping with the level of business.
This tendency has been well substantiated and has
been a major argument in union efforts to increase
penalty pay rates for overtime work. The employer
also has an incentive to hire more skilled, more
productive workers at higher rates of pay in
preference to incurring the same payroll costs for a
larger number of lower-productivity, lower-pay
workers. A shift from pensions and insurance
programs financed by the employer to programs
wholly financed by general taxation would be to
the advantage of low-productivity workers.

Discrimination

Legislation on fair employment practices has
long existed. More recently, the kind of information needed to indicate gross underparticipation of
minorities by occupation, industry, and establishment, such as obtained by the Equal Employment
Opportunity Commission, has become available.
This information should enable the government
better to enforce existing legislation and contract
compliance. The government, in its own employment practices and, lately, through the leverage of
its procurement contracts, has sought to increase
the employment of the disadvantaged. Some of the
government-subsidized, as well as government-
operated, programs for employing and training

low-skill workers (such as NAB–JOBS and the Job Corps), although not explicitly for victims of discrimination, in practice have very high representation of nonwhites and high school dropouts.

Most students of discrimination agree that labor market discrimination in employment and other respects is less important in its effects than the earlier discrimination limiting the education, skill, and employability of the Negro long before he enters the labor market. The measures to eliminate this premarket discrimination are beyond the scope of this survey. Market measures may, however, counteract earlier discrimination to some extent.

In the case of women, discrimination before entry into the labor force is also important, but takes subtler and more pervasive forms. Women are not more poorly educated than men. But they are indoctrinated to regard marriage as their main vocation and to consider only a limited range of occupations as open or appropriate for women. They still concentrate unduly in a few occupations and, thus, keep wages down. If women are to move into the better paid occupations in which men predominate, they must study business, engineering, medicine, etc., in far greater numbers. But there is no concerted effort to persuade women to change their bias in occupational preparation. Women might find it difficult to change until they can see a public commitment to increase female participation in better paid occupations comparable to the current efforts for nonwhites.

Much labor market discrimination results from

ignorance. The use of high school diplomas (or a criterion of sex) as a screening device may have nothing to do with probable performance. But until more reliable techniques are available to employers, such fairly arbitrary procedures will persist.

In terms of discrimination, the most urgent need is more good jobs for Negro males. The one ubiquitous activity which is primarily an employer of males and in which Negroes are greatly underrepresented is construction. This industry also has the advantage that it, in part because it is very well paid for the level of education and training required and level of skill associated with it, is well regarded in terms of prestige. It offers some opportunity for advancement, particularly via subcontracting. Since black females already have very high labor force participation rates, and lower unemployment rates than black males, and for noneconomic reasons as well, the priority is opening up jobs and skills for males, in geographically widespread activities.

Information

The dissemination of information is one way of reducing discrimination which is based on ignorance.[13] But it also improves hiring decisions and the functioning of the labor market. Hiring discrimination based on ignorance can take several forms. One form is the prevalence of stereotyped views of the characteristics of classes of individuals (Negroes, women, teen-agers) as employees which are dubious for any individual member of the class, whatever their validity as statistical generalizations. A second form is a lack of job analysis which results in misconceptions of the worker traits and skills needed for, or compatible with, good job performance. Third is the use of poor predictors of worker performance on the job in making hiring decisions (and in promotion and training selection). The predictors may be unreliable even where relevant aptitudes are identified, if tests for these aptitudes are inappropriate. It often is difficult to determine whether the use of seemingly inappropriate criteria for employment results from ignorance or from discrimination. The outcome may be the same, but the prescription would be different.

The first step in improving the information resources of the employer is outreach. This means that the USTES and various government agencies involved in training and retraining must, themselves, be informed. Their greatest shortcoming is lack of contact with a large proportion of their potential low-skill, low-wage clientele. The second step is obtaining information about employment opportunities through job orders, surveys of job vacancies, and the like. This information, again, is incomplete. Access to such information is less adequate between labor markets than within them. These are all quantitative limitations. But the effectiveness of information also depends on its quality: functional job analysis, realistic specification of requirements for job openings, and proper evaluation of prospective employees, first by the referring agency and then by the prospective employer.

Job Restructuring

Efforts to provide jobs and training for the disadvantaged have met with two contradictory reactions.[14] One is that the jobs obtained are not meaningful; they are dead-end, or lacking in status, or responsibility, or too poorly paid.[15] It is not known how representative this reaction may be. The other reaction is that many of the hard-core unemployed recruited for various job openings and training programs are not amenable to training. They lack the educational background and elementary skills to benefit from conventional training programs, or they lack motivation or incentives.[16] Perhaps these two reactions do not refer to quite the same group of people. Possibly, most of the demand for job "enrichment" is a trickle down from the legion of labor force entrants with college training who still regard their sheepskin as a testament of rare talent and training. But to the extent that these two reactions are representative and correct, they complicate the problem of restructuring jobs to fit the capabilities of low-skill, low-productivity workers. Are jobs to be restructured to fit the present capabilities of the unemployed, or to meet their expectations?

Part of the need for job restructuring does not derive from any limitations of low-skill workers.

Restructuring is a response to a need for incentives. Many of the unemployed are not willing to undergo training programs without assurance of a job at the end. Those whose need for training may be greatest, who require remedial education as well as job-specific training, are least likely to enter, much less stick through the necessary education and training program. To reach them, jobs must come first and training later. In this respect, job restructuring may be regarded as a substitute for formal training programs. By breaking down a relatively complex job into simpler components, job restructuring may provide both immediate placement and also limited career advancement opportunities.

Job restructuring may have as its objective creating openings that are within the capabilities of low-wage workers, or for which they can be trained. It may also, or instead, provide motivation. Many low-skill workers pass up jobs, or quit them, because the jobs are too routine, too tedious and unchallenging, as well as dead-end. Restructuring may make many jobs more palatable and may also create opportunities for career advancement which can render even boring tasks more acceptable.

Creating opportunities for career advancement typically involves much more than the restructuring of jobs that can be filled by low-skill, low-productivity workers. It may require restructuring of an entire industry or occupational hierarchy, such as medical care. Nurses and physicians' assistants may take over many of the functions now reserved for physicians, opening up, in turn, new tasks for nurses aides and other less-skilled personnel.

Many economic opportunities for job restructuring exist (quite apart from the needs and expectations of low-productivity workers). Occupations, like productive processes, become routinized with the passage of time, and some of their bundle of functions become specialized and delegated to less-skilled workers. The health professions, doctors and nurses, may be the most important examples, but opportunities exist in most occupations commonly certified and licensed, as well as in teaching and related educational activities. Some unexploited opportunities result from a lag in regulations or administration, others from monopolistic restraints on entry which are reinforced by defensive preempting of functions. To the extent that demand for low-productivity workers is a constraint on their employment, job restructuring is an important way of relaxing this constraint. Low-productivity workers may benefit directly, or indirectly, as job openings are created by other workers moving up to restructured higher-skill jobs. In the case of health occupations, government facilities have taken the lead in providing training and employment opportunities for technicians and aides. Public funds (through supplier certification for receiving medicaid payments, for instance) could be used to encourage, or at least not discourage, such progress.

To what extent are the very functions involved in an industry—its productive processes—dependent on the supply and price of labor skills? To what extent is the set of tasks involved in a productive process capable of being reassembled into new job contents, bringing job and occupational requirements more into line with the changing level and distribution of education and skills? In the short run, perhaps man must conform to machines and assembly lines. In the longer run, however, these may be redesigned better to fit man. This redesigning may not follow from productivity considerations in the narrow sense of the term, but may become necessary to obtain adequate supplies of labor in an affluent society with discretionary time, income, and labor.

Job restructuring to improve employment and pay may also be tailored to specific handicaps. Illness and disability limit labor force participation, employment, and productivity. A distinction should be made between permanent handicaps which eliminate or limit certain functions, and sickness and poor health which hamper the performance of any function. A handicap is relative to the function to be performed. Very few handicapped workers, even the most severely handicapped, can be said to be unemployable. Their handicap simply means either reduced productivity in their work, or more likely, a narrower choice of jobs in which their disabilities are not a handicap (or not a serious handicap). The problem is the finding of the appropriate jobs (or their creation through restructuring of functions around individual handicaps), and providing the appropriate training for such jobs. Jobs do exist for the blind, the armless, and other severely handicapped individuals.

Resort to sheltered workshops or the issuing of disabled worker certificates which allow payment of less than the minimum wage is a second-best strategy. Undoubtedly, many disabled workers may choose nonparticipation in the labor force, or unemployment, to work paying less than the federal minimum.

The job strategies assume that everything that reasonably may be done by medical technology to overcome handicaps will be done. Job strategies for the handicapped provide that those who need medical care will have it and they provide proper coordination between delivery of medical services and training and job placement assistance. This service is clearly individually tailored. Its requirements are reasonably well approximated by the Rehabilitation Services Administration.[17] Many who might benefit from this service, however, are not reached.

A final potential role for job restructuring has reference to low-wage workers in part-time and short-term employment. The scope for improvement depends on the involuntary nature of the part-time or short-term employment on one hand, and the nature of demand for labor, on the other. Some of this employment is moonlighting by workers who already have a full-time job; much part-time employment is accepted by other workers who do not want a full-time job. The employer's requirements for increasing productivity and pay involve changes in the work schedule which the employee is unwilling to accept. Part-time workers tend to be more costly in terms of space, equipment, and supervision than full-time workers and they have higher turnover rates. If these characteristics exist, then there is not much incentive to invest in training, in more productive equipment, or in other methods of raising the productivity of part-time workers; there is more incentive to raise the productivity of full-time workers.

In addition to part-time employment, short-term employment at the choice of the employee is another situation in which productivity and pay may be low, and the incentives for raising them may not exist, because they involve a change in the work commitment of the employee. When raising incentives is undertaken, it is associated with decasualizing labor and with shifts in employment to full-time employees which deprives the part-time, short-term employees of work opportunities. The question is the degree to which society, and the employer, ought to be allowed to adjust work schedules to meet the needs of such unusual would-be employees, even though such adjustment implies lower productivity and pay and fewer full-time, long-term jobs.

Regional Development

Surplus low-skill labor is geographically concentrated as is low-wage manufacturing industry and low-productivity agriculture. Wages are lower in low-wage industries in the areas with surplus low-skill labor and a high concentration of low-wage manufacturing and low-productivity farming. A regional development policy that will absorb the surplus labor and also provide more better-paid employment opportunities is one strategy for improving the position of low-wage workers. It cannot help many of them since they are to be found in all areas and regions, including areas not eligible for regional development assistance.

Such regional development strategy is part of the program of the Appalachian Regional Commission and of the Economic Development Administration. Creating more jobs is not, however, the dominant focus. EDA is concerned with depressed areas characterized by high unemployment, although they may be high-wage and high-income areas, as well as with underdeveloped areas with a high proportion of low-wage workers and underemployment. The Appalachian Region includes both types of areas. Both programs provide financial assistance for a wide variety of projects contributing to the development of designated areas and improved conditions of the people living in them. Their emphasis is on greater productivity and better jobs, rather than exclusively on more jobs.

"Regional" programs concentrating on central cities, on the other hand, place much greater emphasis on employing the unemployed, on job creation, and less on improving the earnings and occupation and industry composition of the low-wage workers living in central cities.

The fundamental objection to U.S. regional

development programs is that they focus on selected regions and not on the nation, and that,
consequently, an uncertain proportion of their
redistribution of resources to designated disadvantaged areas is to the detriment of national output
and productivity. Resources are transferred from
areas where they are more productive to areas
where they are less productive. There is doubt
about the permanency of the benefits accruing to
many designated areas. Government assistance
may only postpone or slow down a decline that is
inevitable and that is, in the long run, in the
national interest. Because of the long time periods
involved in the sequence from public investment
to induced private investment and resulting economic progress, it is premature to judge the effects
of existing programs.[18] It will always be difficult to
isolate the long run effects of modest government
programs on regional economic conditions.

The alternatives are national, rather than regional, development and migration from low-income regions rather than development assistance.
These alternatives are not simply competitive in
their claims on resources; they are in sharp
conflict. Implementation of one policy can hamper
implementation of the other. Migration may under-
mine economic viability of a community. Investments made in a low-income area are investments
not made elsewhere. These alternatives, therefore,
are not additive in their effects but tend to be
mutually exclusive. There is something to be
learned from other nations, some of which have
placed regional development policy in a national

setting, and whose assistance to low-productivity workers and to the unemployed in lagging regions include migration and resettlement assistance, which so far has proved politically unpalatable in the United States. Present policies compensate for interregional disequilibrium arising from relative immobility of resources by subsidizing, in designated areas, fuller utilization of such resources, including low-productivity labor.

Raising Industry Productivity

If the industrial distribution of low-wage workers is a key correlate of low wages, as it appears to be, then policies to raise wages would include industrial redistribution of labor supply and increased productivity of low-wage industries. There is no question that interindustry, interoccupation mobility is a main source of improving earnings of low-wage workers. It is not so obvious that increasing productivity of low-wage industries will significantly affect the pay of their employees. Productivity improvement attained through major changes in the production process may involve substantial changes in the skill mix, with reduced employment among low-wage, low-skill workers, and increased employment of other workers. Mobility of low-wage workers to higher skills within the plant and industry may not be easy. At the very least, it would require substantial training efforts.

If productivity improvement is attained without adverse effects on the employment prospects of low-wage workers, the second question is whether such gains will be passed on to workers via wage increases, or will take the form of lower prices and/or higher profits instead. The answer depends partly on the industry structure and partly on the organization of labor in the industry. Typically, low-wage industries are not concentrated; they are highly competitive; they have large numbers of small or medium size firms. Typically, the extent of labor organization is low. On all counts, one might expect most of the gains from higher productivity to pass on to consumers through lower prices, with some gains, particularly in the short run, to owners via higher returns on investment. A recent study of four-digit manufacturing industries found that, indeed, there was no significant correlation between increases in average employee compensation and rates of increase in value added per manhour for the period 1954–63.[19] If this is true for all manufacturing, one would believe it to be even truer for low-wage industries. Fuchs has found the same lack of correlation between productivity gains and wage gains in trade and services.[20] For instance, the rate of increase in pay in barbershops, 3.9 percent, was the highest of eighteen service industries between 1948 and 1963, but it was third from the bottom in increase in real output per man, 0.3 percent. Textiles, with much more rapid gains in productivity than apparel, shows nearly the same trend as apparel in average hourly earnings of production workers.

If productivity increase is not "embodied" in higher skills with correspondingly higher wages, but is the result of improved organization, better equipment, etc., the rise in wages is a function of the bargaining power of labor—its organizational strength—and the range of discretion for management, a function of the competitive pressure to which it is subject. Productivity gains not passed on to the customer are most favorable toward wage increases but least favorable toward industry employment. Inelastic demand for the product minimizes employment declines associated with productivity gains without price reductions. Elastic demand is most favorable to expanding employment when prices fall.

Increases in national productivity will be of indirect benefit to low-wage workers. There is no a priori reason to believe that low-wage workers will benefit more, or sooner, if the gain is made in a low-wage industry instead of in a high-wage industry, unless there is monopoly power in the low-wage industry. There is no a priori reason to believe that gains in productivity are more cheaply bought in low-wage than in high-wage industries.

In sum, policies to raise demand for low-productivity workers offer better prospects than policies limited to raising wages. The policies that are most promising are inducements to employers of low-wage workers to encourage on-the-job training and to reduce discrimination in employment; antidiscrimination policies in behalf of nonwhites and particularly of women; and job restructuring modifying occupational demand more in line with capabilities and aspirations of low-productivity labor.

Policies Affecting the Supply of Low-Skill Workers

The earnings of low-wage workers may be increased by reducing the supply of low-skill workers, as well as by raising the demand for them. Reduction in supply can be accomplished by education and training. If education and training are carried out on a sufficient scale, they will reduce the wage differential between skilled and unskilled workers and will lead to some substitution of skilled for less skilled workers on the demand side. Some newly skilled workers will gain. The position of workers remaining unskilled will depend on (a) the responsiveness of wage differentials to changes in the supply of skills and (b) the responsiveness of demand by skill and occupation to changes in wage differentials.

Acquisition of skills by itself may accomplish little unless (a) shortages of skills constraining demand are very large, or (b) demand is very responsive to changes in relative wages. There may have to be a shift in demand, for given relative wages, or college graduates will be working as common laborers. A distinction should be made between general gains in productivity, which increase wages for everyone, and changes in the composition of demand directly affecting the employment and wages of low-productivity workers, which may involve no gain in productivity.

Immigration

Immigration for many years has had minimal

impact on the wages and employment of low-skill workers. Its impact has been further reduced by the shift from country quotas to occupational criteria and by requirements for Department of Labor certification for issuance of work permits. Certification implies that the immigrant worker will not affect wages or employment of citizens adversely. The termination of the bracero program has eliminated adverse effects on farm labor. International commuting is a minor issue and highly localized. Thus, the supply restrictions on low-skill labor that make sense involve training and migration from labor-surplus areas, not restrictions on international migration.

Labor Force Participation of Women

Increasing the supply of low-skill labor by raising the labor force participation rate for women (and teen-agers) in low-income families may seem counterproductive. By itself, it would only raise unemployment rates and exert downward pressure on wages, as long as there are no shortages of low-skill labor. Its objective is to increase employment rather than to raise wages. But to do even the first, it must be complemented by other policies: training, information, and job creation.

The provision of child care facilities on a neighborhood basis has been suggested as a way to increase employment in the central city ghetto. Such a child care system is widely practiced in Europe. It was developed as a deliberate state policy to increase the war labor force in a number of countries. (In the United Kingdom, it was estimated that provision for forty children would release thirty mothers for full-time work and employ eight to ten people.)[21]

In the United States the objective would be not to maximize labor force participation in order to increase national output, but to facilitate full-time labor force participation among women who would choose to participate but find it impossible at present because of lack of child care facilities or because available facilities are inconvenient in location or too expensive. Neighborhood child care facilities would have the additional advantage of creating jobs in low-income neighborhoods for women with limited skill, offering both the income and status which jobs as domestics cannot offer. What is suggested, then, is an institutionalization of a major part of domestic service, obtaining economies of scale and specialization.

With neighborhood child care centers, mothers need not leave their jobs upon childbirth. They need not interrupt their employment history. They become better candidates for hiring, training, and promotion. Nevertheless, it should be repeated that increased availability of low-skill women for work does not per se generate additional demand but tends to depress wages. Child care centers in poverty neighborhoods, at least initially, require public subsidy. This policy can only be recommended as part of a package including training and placement.

Geographic Mobility

Migration is an important way in which local imbalances of labor supply and demand are corrected, whereby individuals succeed in advancing in income and occupation. But the migration patterns of many low-skill workers are inefficient; their processes of relocation are also inefficient. The ratio of gross to net migration is high; there is much reverse migration. And possibly the rates of migration for some low-wage groups are too low.

One requirement for migration is information, which is inversely (though loosely) related to distance. Since low-wage workers depend predominantly on informal sources—relatives and friends—their migration patterns have biases unrelated to differential opportunity and the migrants have the handicaps of inadequate information. They need more and better information that is not subject to the locational, industrial, and occupational biases of their informal social networks.

A second deterrent to the low-wage worker is the cost of migration, in particular the living expenses at the new location before finding a job and getting paid. The cost of migration is high relative to income because many low-wage workers migrate to search for a job rather than to take one, facing expenses without income for an uncertain period. This cost again biases their migration toward paths taken by their relatives and friends so that they can economize on living costs until they find employment.

An information and economic alternative to the network of relatives and friends is a condition to increase and rationalize migration. Since the one way to locate most individuals who may need such an alternative is through applications for unemployment compensation, the USTES must be, at the very least, the referring agency.

An effective migration assistance policy must include information on jobs and financial support until earnings begin. Although this information is sufficient in some cases, it is unproductive in others because successful migration itself involves change of occupation and industry, as well as a new employer. Training and migration are highly complementary.[22]

Farming, in particular, has too much labor, and large numbers migrate from farming every year. But large numbers also return, with net outmigration a small proportion of gross. The large reverse migration, the importance of moonlighting, with its geographical constraints, as a stepping stone to mobility from farming, and the crowding of migrants into low-skill low-wage occupations off-farm, suggest that much farm–nonfarm mobility must take place in two stages. Only after the first stage are the ex-farm workers likely to come within reach of training and referral and placement agencies.

Experimental labor mobility projects begun by the Department of Labor in 1965 are the one federal effort to finance the costs of moving. Their limited success strongly suggests the need for closer association between migration assistance and counselling and placement and the need for follow-ups for maximum effectiveness.[23]

Information

The need for information is not limited to migrants. Lack of information is demonstrated by what seems random mobility among low-wage workers who change jobs, occupations, and industries with little, if any, improvement in their position. Labor market information alone cannot do much for the unskilled worker. It may allow him to reduce the frequency and duration of unemployment experience, but his hourly earnings will still be low. The greatest potential for improvement lies elsewhere: in guiding the individual not into jobs but into occupations and careers.

The United States Training and Employment Service has greatly expanded its functions, from simple referral in response to employer requests, to guidance functions such as referral to training programs, the operation of youth opportunity centers, experimental labor mobility projects, rehabilitation services, and apprenticeship information centers.[24] While this expansion of functions has brought it into closer contact with schools, the early guidance function is one which cannot be performed adequately by an external agency and must ultimately fall on the schools.

The issues revolving around forecasting of skill requirements, and the use of forecasts, are fundamental. First, there is the sheer difficulty of making forecasts far enough ahead to be truly useful for training and career choices. Second is the even greater difficulty of making these forecasts not on a national basis but on a regional or local basis, to the extent that adequate labor mobility across the nation is not assumed. Third is the question of the use to be made of even the most reliable forecasts. Schools and training facilities may modify their curricula; vocational guidance counselors may adapt their recommendations to the forecasts; students and workers may be guided accordingly. But the responses of thousands of institutions and millions of individuals do not amount to a coherent manpower plan. The aggregate result more often than not is an overresponse that turns shortages into surpluses and vice versa. These overresponses tend to correct themselves, but only over a long time and at a high cost.

The market for skills and careers is not quite like the market for hogs or television sets. We lack both the instruments and the tradition for a national manpower policy that would adjust the output of skills to the expected demand for them. But information alone can do much of the job of minimizing overresponses and maladjustments. Forecasts on demand for skills need to be matched with constantly updated information on the output of skills, so that students, counselors, and workers, if not schools, can anticipate changes in the balance of demand and supply.

Guidance on education, training, and career objectives is most effective before labor force entry. Once an individual becomes a member of the labor force, it is difficult to take the time for corrective education, vocational training, etc. If guidance occurs while the individual is still in school full time, the incremental costs, and the opportunity costs, are much lower.

Education

Individuals with higher educational achievement typically have higher incomes. Therefore, it is often concluded, the solution to the low-productivity problem of some workers is obvious: make sure they get more education. Once individuals are standardized for occupation, the conclusion no longer follows so obviously. Only where education is a prerequisite to qualify for a highly-paid occupation does the widely accepted relation hold unambiguously. Even in these cases, the question for the policymaker is whether educational prerequisites are reasonable, or whether they are simply monopolistic barriers to entry which restrict the supply of workers for a given occupation and raise average earnings. Alternatively, educational attainment may be a simple way of screening large numbers of potential employees, even though, in fact, level of education is uncorrelated with potential performance.

A different hypothesis suggests that educational achievement is correlated with ability, energy, drive, and other qualities that will result in higher incomes for their possessors, regardless of how much education they attain. According to this view, many low-productivity workers are unlikely to benefit appreciably from education because they are deficient in the qualities required for productive work, or even for acquiring high levels of skill and flexibility. For them, a policy of training in specific skills may be productive, whereas a policy of more general educational preparedness is not.[25]

If more education will greatly reduce the number of low-productivity workers, the implication is that expansion of higher-productivity employment is constrained by a lack of adequately educated (trained) workers. The hypothesis need not imply a shortage of workers with modest levels of skill for lack of the necessary educational attainment. It could be compatible with a shortage of highly skilled and professional workers for lack of educational and training attainment of a sufficient proportion of the labor force, and hence a relative overcrowding of occupations requiring less formal education (training). Raising educational and training achievements would permit expansion of the most highly-skilled occupations and would allow workers currently occupying less skilled positions to move up, creating openings as they leave.

Although there are instances of supply constraints on employment that are quantitatively significant, e.g., physicians, there is no evidence that the proportion of the labor force in higher-skill occupations is significantly smaller than it would be if it were not for inadequate education. The evidence to the contrary consists of (1) the fact that average educational attainment of broad occupational groups has been rapidly converging; (2) the fact that average educational attainment has increased much faster than the growth in the em-

ployment share of the higher-skill occupations
(with much of the growth in the professional and
technical group in the last decade attributable to
the increase in teachers, which is ending with the
graduation of children born in the high birthrate
years); and (3) the modest projected increases in
employment share of professional and technical
workers and managers and officials despite the
large educational gains of the recent past.[26]
Johnson concludes that the substitutability between college trained and other labor is high
(elasticity of substitution of 1.3), and he anticipates
a decline in relative returns to college educated
labor because there are too many job categories in

TABLE 19
TRENDS IN EDUCATIONAL ATTAINMENT
BY OCCUPATION

	1948	1972
Professional and technical	16+ years	16.3 years
Managers, proprietors	12.2	12.9
Sales	12.4	12.7
Clerical		12.6
Craftsmen	9.7	12.2
Operatives	9.1	11.6
Service workers	8.7	12.0
Laborers, nonfarm	8.0	11.2
Farmers and farm laborers	8.0	9.4

SOURCE: *Manpower Report of the President*,
1973, p. 180.

which additional education yields no increase in productivity.[27]

The educational revolution is well publicized. Less than 20 percent of an age group now fail to complete high school. The majority of high school graduates receive some college education. What has been little noticed is the associated, and startling, convergence of educational attainment by occupational group.

Since farmers are older, on the average, than other occupational groups, one can expect a rapid closing of the gap from below as they retire or die. Outside farming, in 1972 the median educational attainment by broad occupational groups varied by only 1.7 years, if one excludes professional and technical occupations. In 1948, the range was almost twice as wide—3.2 years. The implication is that schooling is no longer a major discriminant variable between laborers and craftsmen or clerical workers. The dispersion of educational attainment by occupation is much greater than between occupations. The fond hope that high school diplomas will take care of things is foolish.

A diploma still will help in two ways, however. First, in many states vocational training, formerly available in high school, has been deferred to post-high school institutions. A diploma will facilitate access to training. Secondly, many employers use high school diplomas as a screening device, therefore, its possession greatly improves an applicant's chances for a job and for job-related training. But it is the training, not the education, that confers improved earnings and occupational advance.

The near-universality of the high school diploma as a minimum floor for the new generation, and the entirely unprecedented development that the majority of the new generation is now college-bound, ready or not, places a high school dropout in a disadvantageous position in competing for available jobs, whether or not a diploma has any bearing on his ability to perform. The degree may become a first crude sifting device in selecting among job applicants, and individuals with less education will have to compete with individuals who have gone to college.

For women as a group, there is no shortcoming in number of years of school completed. There is a qualitative deficiency: a lack of career orientation in educational specialization, and too great a concentration on a limited range of specializations. More education for nonwhites is necessary for them to achieve greater representation in the highly skilled occupations. But it is not necessary to move most of those in unskilled and semiskilled jobs into better-paying jobs and occupations. There has been little, if any, increase in the average skill of the labor force during a period when its average educational attainment increased spectacularly. There is considerable dispersion in educational attainment within occupations without formal educational prerequisites. Although nonwhites have lower educational attainment than whites in low-wage occupations, in some cases they also have a higher proportion of high school or college graduates. Negroes in most occupations already have a higher average educational attainment than whites had in the same occupations twenty years ago. But many employers specify high school degrees, or more, for jobs that formerly did not call for them (and which do not now call for them in other advanced nations).

When two or more criteria are used in selecting employees, it is whichever significant criterion is least often met—the scarce currency, so to speak—that will determine who gets hired. Awarding nearly everyone a high school diploma will raise unemployment rates among high school graduates without assuring jobs for those who formerly had no diploma. The more selective criterion, likely to be relevant skill or experience, will dominate employer decisions. This is an argument for stressing vocational education and, particularly, on-the-job training, which provide both skills and experience, in preference to stressing additional formal education which will improve the absolute position of the disadvantaged without changing their relative position, and therefore will not much improve their employment or occupational experience.

When the half-truth that the road to affluence is paved with diplomas is generalized from individuals who advance their relative position to the masses that do not, it becomes a grand deception, a fallacy of composition. If everyone has a diploma, then many graduates will be unskilled laborers.

The conclusion is that the most productive strategy encourages employment experience as well as training and such other measures as may increase the chances for such employment experience. It is in this way that low-productivity workers will have their best chance of competing on equal terms with others who have more formal education than they.

Training

Training as a solution to unemployment offers more promise than training as a way of eliminating low wages. For the latter objective assumes changes in the occupational structure away from low-productivity, low-wage jobs. It also requires more training and a better educational foundation.

Training alone is of limited value without good prospects of good jobs ahead. This is a strong reason for emphasizing the advantages of employer-conducted training. The prospect of a job provides incentives for trainees, who are much less likely either to enter or to complete a training program which is disassociated from ensuing placement and work. But many low-wage workers do not have the opportunity to participate. The industries and firms conducting the most training are selective in their hiring choices, and are not hiring many people. Business investment in employee training also means an interest in low turnover. Training by business firms of individuals who are not their employees, on a contract basis, and training conducted by government agencies, can reach workers further on down in the hiring and training queue.

The effectiveness of public programs is limited by the willingness of trainees to participate, which declines with age. According to one survey of men not in the labor force, 72 percent of those aged 25–44 were interested in training, but only 56 percent of those aged 45–54 were interested.[28] Willingness also varies directly with education: only 48 percent of those with less than a high school education were interested in training versus 60 percent of those with high school or more. Participation is influenced by the pay trainees receive, by the assurance of a training-related job at the end of the program, and by the quality of the job. The rate of completion by those starting out is a tricky statistic, since some quit a training program because they get a job before completing it.

Our experience with the diversity of relatively new and experimental programs is too short to draw firm conclusions on the preferred approaches or, more realistically, on the preferred mixes. For, the diverse programs reach different clienteles: the Job Corps is for youth, the Manpower Development and Training Act institutional and on-the-job training programs are for workers of all ages, whereas the Community Action Program and Concentrated Employment Program are primarily for nonwhites.

If we have doubts about the relative efficiency of alternative programs, we are quite unsure about their absolute productivity.[29] The biggest difficulty is with control groups: what would have happened to the trainees if they had not participated? To what extent are the gains of trainees a redistribution of jobs and income from others like themselves; to what extent are they net gains? Yet in the scale conducted to date, no matter how they are measured, returns usually appear high.

The past shortcomings of vocational education

in schools are well known and progress is being made to gear it to the needs of the economy and of different groups of individuals.[30] This means both bridging the transition between school and work and bringing opportunities for skill adaptation and advancement to workers who now lack them.

Perhaps the most difficult problem is that of unrealistic earnings and occupational expectations. What makes them so difficult to modify is that they may not be unrealistic in each case, only in the aggregate. Governor Nelson Rockefeller is reported to have told a group of students that both his grandfathers were high school dropouts but that he could not recommend this particular road to riches for our times. Some high school dropouts will do very well. Many college graduates will get professional and managerial "positions." But many will just get jobs. The supply of educated people at almost every level has been increasing faster than the occupational requirements for education. Yet expectations are based on an absolute relation between occupations and earnings and education which is outdated. The occupational distribution of the demand for labor changes only slowly, and then in response to changes in technology and in final demand, not to worker desires. Education and training policy cannot succeed in eliminating low-skill, low-wage jobs.

Income Maintenance Policies

Income maintenance programs operating outside the labor market are relevant to a discussion of low-productivity workers because they affect the number in the labor force and the amount of labor they are willing to offer at various wage rates, i.e., they affect both the output and distribution objectives.

Income maintenance programs have two kinds of effect on the labor supply. The first depends on the level of income support. The higher this level, the less pressing the need for additional income from work. Higher levels will reduce labor force participation and make eligible recipients more choosy in terms of type of work and wage rates.

The second effect is that of the marginal tax rate on earnings, or the loss of income support payments per given increment in earned income. Until recently, the tax rate on income from AFDC (Aid to Families with Dependent Children) was 100 percent; in most states assistance payments were reduced dollar per dollar with increases in earnings. The higher the level of income support, the larger the annual earnings required to justify working at all. The disincentive effect, however, was more a function of the number of dependents, which determines AFDC payments, than of the wage rate. Until 1962, families headed by an employable male were not eligible for AFDC at all. Since then, however, assistance has been available. However, many families with employable members were eligible for larger amounts under AFDC than they could earn by working. Hausman estimated that 41 percent of the fathers and 73 percent of the mothers receiving AFDC could not reasonably expect to earn more than their assistance income on an annual basis.[31]

The Social Security Act amendments of 1967

reduced the tax rate on earned income for AFDC recipients by providing an earnings exemption of $30 a month plus one-third of the remainder, or a 67 percent marginal tax rate on earnings in excess of $30 a month. This rate is further reduced by allowances for work expenses. Evidence from the WIN program suggests that this modest incentive has had some success in raising earnings and reducing welfare payments of enrollees, but not in increasing the rate at which enrollees move out of welfare.[32] The still very high tax on earnings helps explain why some low-wage workers are unwilling to accept available jobs. If AFDC is an alternative, they have some incentive to work, but not much, if they can only keep one-third of their low-wage earnings, which are subject to tax.

The proposed Family Assistance Act would allow families to earn $720 without reduction in assistance payments, and would have a 50 percent tax rate on amounts earned above $720. Family allowances, as practiced in many countries, would have a zero tax rate: their receipt is unrelated to amount of earned income. Negative income tax proposals, not limited to families with dependent children, would have a variety of tax rates. With tax (negative) rates below 100 percent, there is some incentive to work at any wage rate, and the relative discouragement of part-time and part-year work is eliminated. The higher the tax rate is, the higher the wage needed to net any given amount per hour of work. Therefore, the higher the rate is, the lower the labor force participation will be and the more selective the income support recipients will be as to the type of job and wage rate. This conclusion is weakened, but not refuted, by the fact that a low marginal tax rate is associated with larger income transfers for any given level of earned income. Some families will find the level of income support sufficient to discourage them from working as much as they could, or from working at all.

Income maintenance programs, like government as employer of last resort, exert upward pressure on wages of low-productivity workers and accentuate problems of work discipline. Their expansion could induce employers to economize on the use of such workers. These programs involve some conflict between the goals of output and distribution. Shortly we should have better information, based on experiments conducted in New Jersey, on the labor force participation and earnings effects of various levels of income support and marginal tax rates.

The issue is not simply one of incentives to work, but of incentives to increase earnings, to raise productivity, whether by migration, training, or by other means. With higher levels of income maintenance, and significant rates of reduction in transfers as earned income increases, productivity-enhancing policies might have to offer reasonable prospects of really large increases in income in order to appeal to many low-productivity workers. But since income maintenance programs are geared to family size, they set no absolute minimum as would the federal government as employer of last resort. A high floor will discourage labor force participation in direct relation to size of family and ratio of dependents to potential workers in the family. Negative income taxes, in which adults are considered in determining transfer payments, might be more discouraging to labor force participation than other programs in which only dependent children influence the size of transfers. Any income support program involves a clear conflict between the goals of output and of distribution. Policy can only choose the most favorable exchange rate.

Work disincentives of current proposals have been overemphasized perhaps, because, after all, they would replace existing policies whose disincentive effects are much greater. The marginal effects of negative income tax rates may have been overstressed because some of the disincentive effects may result not from the marginal rate but from the assured minimum income.

Conclusions. The catalogue of options discussed above adds up to a somewhat unpromising outlook. The structure of demand for labor will change slowly, thus limiting the expectations from education and training policies. The prospects that demand for low-skill jobs will rapidly diminish are simply not realistic. Yet the chances of reducing the number of low-wage jobs, of compressing the wage structure from below, are much better than the modest expected changes in demand would suggest.

There is evidence of a shortage of workers for many unskilled job openings. For a variety of reasons, many Americans will not take them even though they have no better job alternatives. They feel that they are capable of something better; that their rising educational attainment qualifies them for something better; that they deserve something better; and income from other sources provides an alternative to work. So we let openings go unfilled, or hire foreigners, or raise the ante. Eventually the main result of reluctance to accept such jobs will be higher pay. There is a rough justice here. We look down on the garbage collector, and then pay for our snobbery. Every time enough of us call policemen pigs, their salaries go up. Conversely, if we puff with pride at our particular prestigious occupation, we soon find it crowded and through increased competition, earnings go down.

Chapter Six
NEEDS FOR INFORMATION

We know a good deal about low-wage workers: who they are, where they live, the industries and occupations in which they are concentrated. There is more to be learned, but we know enough to proceed. We also know a good deal about why their wages are low—the correlation between wages and skill and productivity, the balance between supply and demand in the market for labor. But we do not know enough about the relative importance of the causal and contributory factors in low wages and the factors in high unemployment and low labor participation rates among low-wage workers. And we know little about the results of various policies that have already been tried, much less about others still awaiting experiment. It is in this area that research is most needed: to evaluate existing programs, to reorient policy priorities, to improve programs.

We need more information on the dispersion of wage rates in specific occupations by demographic characteristics in order to discover the extent to which interindustry differences in occupational wages represent quality differences. Research is needed on the influence of size of firm on occupational wages, and research is needed on the nature of intervening variables: scale effects on productivity, capital per worker, training inputs.

We need a better understanding of the persistence of low-wage industries. What has been the effect of post–World War II migration from farming on wages and unemployment in low-wage industries and occupations? What has been the effect of rising labor force participation rates for married women? Of the increase in share of nonwhites in the urban labor force? What is the relation between labor supply, capital per worker, and low wages? Do money wage differentials by size of city, and between regions, reflect real wage differentials, or are they partly explainable in terms of cost of living, or in terms of amenity or "benefit of living" differentials?

Declining low-wage industries are largely employers of males, whereas expanding ones are not. What role has this shift, in particular, migration from agriculture, played in labor force participation of women? How important is the concentration of women in a very limited range of occupations in depressing wages in them? How much of this concentration is the result of discrimination on the demand side or how much is a result of occupational preferences on the supply side—a "distaff culture"?

The striking increase in teen-age unemployment rates, especially of nonwhite high school dropouts, needs understanding. Does it represent efficient and valuable learning behavior, or a poorly-functioning labor market for badly-informed workers, a wasteful transition from school to work? What is the role of weak motivation, of unrealistic expectations of work and income, and poor work attitudes, in inducing such unfavorable labor market experience? Assuming that much of the increase in teen-age unemployment is the result of the growth of teen-agers as a proportion of the labor force, can we expect a decline in teen-age unemployment rates with the current reversal in demographic trends?

The position of nonwhites raises both research and policy problems. Why have unemployment rates risen relative to those of whites? Why is the occupational mix of nonwhites much worse in the 26 million workers sample of the Equal Employment Opportunity Commission than in the labor force as a whole? Is this unfavorable composition attributable to underrepresentation of services and trade in the sample, or to marked differences between very small establishments and other establishments in the employment and promotion of nonwhites, or in occupational composition? What are the facts about the significant percentage of nonwhite unskilled and semiskilled workers with high school diplomas or better?

Labor force participation rates pose several riddles. Why have they declined for adult males? Why has there been a sharp rise in nonparticipation among young nonwhites not enrolled in

school? What is the explanation for the positive
relation between education and labor force participation of married women? Is it the education, or
the wider job options available to educated
women, or the associated higher earnings?

Americans have a naive faith in technological
solutions to all problems. But it is not clear how
much of the problem of low-productivity workers
is amenable to technological approaches. How big
a gap is there between income and occupational
expectations among low-skill workers and the labor
market offer? How important is this gap in raising
unemployment rates and lowering labor force
participation rates? How many jobs are unskilled,
routine, and offering the holder no ladder of
advancement, either occupationally or organiza-
tionally? What are the capabilities to move up of
those who occupy routine jobs? To what extent is
the demand for challenge, responsibility, interest,
and meaning in the job to be found among low-
skill workers? How realistic is that demand in
terms of their capabilities? How realistic is it in
terms of the occupational structure of the labor
market? To what extent is the dissatisfaction with
low-wage jobs a demand for permanent upward
mobility and to what extent is it a demand
satisfiable by modest upgrading early in the individual's working life, with no prospect of further
advancement ahead?

We need more knowledge of the complex
process of skill acquisition and upgrading, training
and promotion carried out by business and industry; of their costs and effectiveness; and of the
hiring and selection criteria which ration out these

opportunities to workers. To what extent do hiring subsidies and training subsidies lead to lasting improvements in employment experience and wages of those hired and trained? How successfully can we develop more reliable tests for predicting work performance in thousands of low-skill jobs? How successfully can we disseminate these tests among employers and have them displace more traditional methods of selection?

What are low-wage industry responses to large increases in low-skill employee wages? How much of their response would take the form of a change in industry occupational mix, and how much upgrading of low-skill labor currently employed would be feasible?

What would be the response of low-productivity workers to various alternative income maintenance schemes? What would be the effect of government assumption of the role of employer of last resort on labor force participation, employment, unemployment, and wages?

Finally, we need a hardheaded look at the essential educational requirements for various skills in the labor force and a look at workers' present quantitative and qualitative shortcomings. Of the three major policies on the supply side, education, training, and migration, how much can each accomplish? How much can they accomplish in conjunction? How much of each would be needed to reach its maximum potential contribution to raising wages and labor force participation and reducing unemployment rates among low-productivity workers?

Chapter Seven
SUMMARY AND
CONCLUSIONS

Concern with low-productivity workers has two bases: the level of output and the distribution of income. In practice, we are concerned with low-wage workers, although low wages are not identical with low productivity or low skill. Low skill is a personal attribute preventing full development of individual potentials. Low productivity may be a characteristic of industry and occupation that detracts from maximization of output. Low wages, on the other hand, may violate our concepts of equity.

The definition of low-wage workers is arbitrary, except from a policy standpoint. If the definition includes a significant proportion of the labor force, policy prescriptions must emphasize the demand side, whereas policies on the supply side may be able to cope with small numbers of low-wage workers.

The facts about low-wage workers are reasonably clear. The lowest-wage, and also rapidly declining, sector is agriculture. A high proportion of low-wage workers is found in nearly all retail trades, in private household employment, in most service groups, notably in hotels and other lodging places, laundry and cleaning establishments, motion picture theaters, and hospitals. Manufacturing is a high-wage sector, but some industry groups have a high proportion of low-wage workers, the most important being textiles, apparel, lumber and wood products, and furniture and fixtures. Most workers in these sectors are not low-wage, however, and low-wage workers are to be found in most industries.

By occupation, low-wage workers form a high proportion of farmers, farm and nonfarm laborers, private household workers, other service workers, and operatives. Low-wage workers, however, are to be found in most occupations, and many workers even in the lowest-wage occupations are not low-wage. Neither industry nor occupation is a good criterion for differentiating between low-wage and other workers.

The South has lower wages than the non-South by every measure, but differentials are much greater for Negroes than for whites, for low-skill than for skilled occupations, for trade and services than for manufacturing. Average earnings by occupation and by industry are also positively related to city size. Differentials cannot be attributed to industry or occupational mix, although the former contributes. So does the high proportion of Negroes and their unfavorable occupational distribution.

The most significant demographic correlates of

low wages are low educational attainment (less than high school), nonwhite race, female sex, and youth. A disproportionate number of low-wage workers are secondary family workers, most of whom are females, many very young. Low wages are also correlated with high unemployment rates, with low labor force participation rates in most cases, but also with high rates of dual job holding.

Although teen-agers as a group are low-wage workers, there are sharp differences in occupational distribution between high school dropouts and graduates. High teen-ager unemployment rates largely reflect labor force entry and reentry, a casual attachment which drops sharply for married teen-agers and with age. High rates have been accentuated by the growth (now ending) of teen-agers as a proportion of the labor force.

Women reveal almost as great an occupational concentration in 1970 as in 1900. Females are typically overrepresented in low-wage industries as well as occupations (farming excepted). But females have lower average wages than males in the same detailed occupations as well as in the same industries.

Negroes and workers of Spanish surname are also concentrated in low-wage occupations and industries, have lower earnings than whites by occupation, lower occupational position by industry and by educational attainment, and higher unemployment.

The correlation between education and income is largely attributable to the relation between education and occupation. Variations of education within occupations are not associated with large differences in income. Low wages and adverse occupational distribution among nonwhites (but not among women) are partially attributable to low educational attainment. However, educational differences between occupations are rapidly diminishing.

All indices of disability, poor health, and work limitations have a higher incidence among those not in the labor force than among those in it, and a higher incidence among the unemployed than the employed. These indices are also inversely related to income and to occupational level. Differences among women, however, are much smaller than among men.

To an unknown extent, high unemployment rates and low labor force participation rates among low-skill workers result from an unwillingness to take the low-status, poorly paid jobs available to them. To some extent, poor employment experience results from behavioral patterns of some low-skill workers that are characteristic of a "culture of poverty."

Factors contributing to the condition of low-wage workers include discrimination by employers. For women and teen-agers it is difficult to quantify the extent of economically unjustified discrimination, since their high turnover and other characteristics justify some employer preference. But for Negroes the effects are measurable and large. The occupational concentration of women, which is partly, but by no means entirely, the result of employer sex-labelling of jobs, depresses wages and hinders occupational advancement. Much of the damage done by discrimination, both against nonwhites and against women, occurs before entry into the labor force.

Except in agriculture, there is no evidence of a general decline in demand for low-skill labor. Low-wage trades and services have experienced slow growth in productivity and substantial growth in employment. The picture is more mixed in low- wage manufacturing. Advancing technology destroys low-skill and high-skill jobs alike, and creates new ones. Its effect in raising the average skill of the employed has been small at best.

Adverse factors and trends, therefore, must be found mainly on the supply side. The impact of immigration has been small; that of foreign agricultural labor has been practically eliminated. Impacts of Mexican border commuters are local. Puerto Rican migration to New York adversely affected the migration of Negroes and the trend in apparel industry wage differentials between New York and the rest of the country. The influx of Cubans to Miami temporarily raised local area unemployment rates. The major effects on the low-wage labor from the supply side are migration from agriculture, the sharp rise in labor force participation of married women, and the increase in the Negro and teen-ager share of the population of working age. The dramatic increase in the proportion of the population finishing high school and going to college has differentiated the high school dropout much more sharply from the rest of the economically active population.

To a limited extent, high unemployment and low wages result from inadequate functioning of the labor market. Secondary family workers are geographically immobile; many have part-time or part-year work preferences which may be difficult to satisfy. Mobility among low-wage workers seems adequate but inefficient. Too much mobility from agriculture is unsuccessful, judging by the relation between gross and net migration. Too many jobless low-skill workers move to search for work with inadequate sources of information. Low-skill workers show high quit rates, partly due to low wages, but their quitting results too infrequently in occupational improvement.

Unemployment rate differentials by skill remain large within the same labor market. Wage differentials have been constrained in a number of ways from performing their equilibrating function: by legal minimum wages, rigidities introduced by collective bargaining, and worker unwillingness to adjust wages to labor surplus conditions. Improved alternatives to earned income have facilitated rigidity. As a result, differential unemployment and labor force participation rates have had to bear a disproportionate share of labor market adjustment burdens.

Policies may be aimed at wages directly or indirectly through changing supply of and/or demand for low-wage workers. A policy of raising minimum wages responds to symptoms, not causes. It cannot raise real wages of low-productivity workers for long, and entails disemployment effects for some as a result of employer responses to higher labor costs. There is more scope for raising wages in local market industries, e.g., retail trade and most low-wage services, than in industries competing in regional and national markets. Wages may be increased in public service with less adverse effects on employment than when they are raised in competitive markets. Financing must be largely federal, to avoid raising unduly the cost of the local environment for other industries comprising the economic base of the community.

The case for reducing minimum wages, whether statutory, union-imposed, or socially prescribed, is in terms of reducing unemployment only. It is weak, but may merit a trial for teenagers. Many unemployed are unwilling to accept jobs paying the minimum wage. The availability of income alternatives to such jobs makes the payoff from an even lower minimum distinctly unpromising.

On the demand side, improvements in net foreign trade position could raise employment and wages in low-wage industries. Government discretion is limited to restricting imports—other countries can counteract export–subsidy programs. Low-wage industry labor is already heavily protected by tariffs and informal quotas, without which employment would drop and trends would be adversely affected. Additional protection would come at a high and increasing cost.

Employment and training of low-productivity workers may be subsidized by tax credits or by reimbursement for extra expenses incurred. It is desirable to avoid simple transfer of jobs (and

unemployment) from one group of low-wage
workers to another, and to avoid paying for what
employers might have done on their own anyway.
Government as employer of last resort avoids the
problem of determining employee selection criteria and the proper compensation for business. It
can increase demand for the hard-to-employ, rather
than transferring demand from other low-skill
workers. It faces the conflict between the two
objectives of productivity and avoidance of competition with business. Whatever wage is paid by
government becomes a universal minimum. Finally, government may encourage employers to
hire high-risk workers, and/or locate in high-risk
areas, by bearing the excess risks and uncertainties
itself. All these policies must resolve conflicts
between national productivity and distribution
criteria.

Government, through legislation, through its
own employment practices, and through its power
as purchaser and grantor, seems to be doing most
of the right things to prevent or counter discrimination on the basis of race. How much further it
should carry these measures is debatable. Less is
being done about discrimination against women.

Some discrimination in hiring, training, and
promotion is based on ignorance of the qualities
required for a job or use of bad predictors of
expected performance. Improvement of job analysis, personnel evaluation, and predictors of corre-
spondence between the two, plus improved referral of low-wage workers, can increase
employment, wages, and opportunities for ad-

vancement of low-productivity workers. But to a considerable extent it is necessary, or most efficient, to restructure jobs to the capabilities and needs of low-skill workers. Job restructuring offers incentives to work and to accept training. Opportunities exist especially in services and public employment.

Since the concentrations of low-wage regions, industries, and individuals largely overlap, development policies for regions can prove helpful. But they risk sacrificing national growth gains for redistribution of public and private investment resources to typically unpromising areas, slowing adjustment.

National development, increasing the productivity of the economy, will help the low-wage worker indirectly. But productivity gains in low-wage industries need not increase wages for low-productivity workers. Changes in production functions and associated changes in occupational structure require training and retraining for continued employability of low-skill workers in the industry. Gains in low-wage industry productivity are more likely to result in a decline in its product prices relative to other prices than in a wage increase relative to other industries.

The payoffs from policies modifying demand for low-productivity workers seem much higher than from policies that just raise wages. Training subsidies, job restructuring, and reduction of discrimination appear to offer substantial benefits.

On the side of supply, increased labor force participation rates of low-productivity workers can be brought about by improvements in their health, improved labor market information and guidance services, and through provision of child-care facilities. But increased participation rates only raise unemployment and depress wages unless accompanied by appropriate job development, training, and placement efforts.

Employment can be increased by migration from labor surplus to labor shortage areas. Low-wage workers need a substitute for friends and relatives both as the dominant source of information about jobs, and for assistance until they are earning. This dependence biases their migration patterns and restricts their options to the low-wage jobs about which their contacts are most likely to be knowledgeable.

The more pressing needs for information, however, are in guiding training programs, career choices, and occupational moves. To be most effective, such guidance should come in school, before entry into the labor force.

Although education may bring rich rewards for individuals, it is no panacea. Converting everyone into a high school graduate will not revolutionize the occupational composition of the employed labor force—it will only change the educational attainment of low-wage workers. Training has the same limitation; it cannot convert everyone into a skilled well-paid employee because that is not the composition of the labor demand, although it is changing slowly. Overqualification can eliminate supply restraint on changing demand for labor in the direction of higher skills. Overqualification will tend to reduce skill–wage differentials, inducing more rapid shifts from low-skill to high-skill labor demand. But it will also build up frustrations.

Training is more pertinent than high school education for low-productivity workers, in terms of the objective requirements for jobs, although the widespread tendency to use a high school diploma as a screening device warns us not to neglect formal qualifications. Training and related experience are likely to become far more important selection criteria in hiring decisions than incremental formal education in a society where nearly everyone finishes high school, and more than half the college-age group starts college. Incremental years of formal education have rising opportunity costs in that work experience and training are foregone.

A higher floor on income for those not working will adversely affect motivation to work for some. On the other hand, further reductions in the marginal tax on earnings of those on welfare, now one-third, will improve work incentives. The net effect on labor force participation and employment is difficult to judge, since it depends on two opposing influences, both uncertain in magnitude.

The diversity of problems requires a multiplicity of solutions. But most low-wage jobs do not constitute an economic pathology in any sense, nor are the holders of these jobs to be regarded as problems. They merely reflect an equilibrium system of wage differentials under properly functioning demand and supply conditions.

Most of the policies which have been mentioned are not alternatives, strictly speaking. The dominant relation is, rather, one of complementarity. The success of a training program may have been contingent on adequate investment to utilize the skills. The law of diminishing returns is bound to come into operation sooner or later for any policy. The scale of experiment is crucial in determining the productivity of the instrument. A training policy, which may prove very successful on a small scale, may fail when conducted for all low-skill workers. Trainees are no longer selected on bases conducive to success, and the increment to the supply of skills may be so large as to exceed available demand.

To bring about adjustment in demand and supply it is sufficient for a small proportion of the supply to migrate or to change industry or occupation. Lack of mobility in any of these dimensions by most low-wage workers is not a concern as long as enough workers move to bring about appropriate adjustments. On the other hand, if the equilibrium wage rate and unemployment rate differentials between low-skill workers and others are not acceptable, then measures must be taken directly affecting all, not only a small proportion of, low-productivity workers. If we accept the market system of allocation, then redistributive considerations are largely relegated to extramarket measures.

In a properly functioning market system, there will be substantial wage differentials, reflecting differences in demand and supply conditions of

TABLE 20
A SUMMARY OF THE PROBLEMS OF LOW-WAGE WORKERS AND APPROPRIATE POLICIES

Problems	Policies
1. formal education as a routine job-entry requirement	1. change in hiring standards
2. formal education as a necessary foundation for vocational training	2. reduce high school dropout rate; provide adult remedial education
3. lack of skill	3. training, vocational education; restructure jobs to fit worker limitations
4. skill not in demand in the locality	4. migration and/or retraining
5. skill in oversupply nationally	5. retraining
6. unavailability for full-time or for continuous employment	6. restructure work schedules; make normal work schedule possible through child care centers
7. poor health, disability	7. medical treatment, vocational rehabilitation
8. geographical immobility	8. regional development
9. lack of information about jobs, training programs	9. vocational guidance, employment services
10. unwillingness to accept available openings	10. training to qualify for better jobs, change attitudes, engender realistic expectations
11. lack of expected work attitudes and behavior patterns	11. education and training
12. high risk to employers	12. government compensation, underwriting of risk
13. exploitation by monopsonists	13. labor organization, enforcement of competition

(Continued on page 214)

TABLE 20 (Continued)

Problems	Policies
14. low-productivity industry	14. investment, research
15. employer discrimination	15. collection of information, enforcement of laws, government employment and procurement policies
16. low-wage foreign competition	16. tariffs, quotas
17. insufficient local demand for labor	17. regional development, migration
18. employer ignorance about job requirements, employee performance predictors	18. better job analysis and better personnel selection and training procedures

labor of varying skill, education, experience, and location. As long as "low" wages are defined in relation to average wages, and as long as "poverty" is defined in terms of average incomes, there is no way to eliminate them (although large reductions are possible and desirable within the market system) without doing violence to the system of labor allocation which we now have.

The problems of low-wage workers and relevant policies are summarized in Table 20.

Notes

Chapter One

1. U.S. Bureau of the Census, *Income in 1967 of Families in the United States*, Current Population Reports, Series P–60, no. 59 (Washington: Government Printing Office, April 18, 1969), pp. 2, 33. Elizabeth Waldman and Yvonne C. Olson, "Unemployment in the American Family," *Monthly Labor Review*, October 1968, pp. 42.

2. Carl Rosenfeld and Vera C. Perrella, "Why Women Start and Stop Working: A Study in Mobility," *Monthly Labor Review*, September 1965, p. 1078.

3. Elizabeth Waldman, "Marital and Family Characteristics of Workers, March 1966," *Monthly Labor Review*, April 1968, p. 35.

Chapter Three

1. Paul O. Flaim, "Persons Not in the Labor Force: Who They Are and Why They Don't Work," *Monthly Labor Review*, July 1969, pp. 3–13. Harvey Hilaski, "Unutilized Manpower in Poverty Areas of Six U.S. Cities," *Monthly Labor Review*, December 1971, pp. 45–52.

2. United States Department of Labor, Bureau of Labor Statistics, *Employee Compensation in the Private NonFarm Economy, 1968* Bulletin no. 1722 (Washington, D.C.: Government Printing Office, 1971). Steven Sternlieb and Alvin Bauman, "Employment Characteristics of Low-Wage Workers," *Monthly Labor Review*, July 1972, pp. 9–14.

3. George E. Delehanty and Robert Evans, Jr., "Low-Wage Employment: An Inventory and an Assessment." Mimeographed, Cambridge (?): M.I.T. (?), 1969.

4. Delehanty and Evans also studied the distribution of average wages by state, establishing as an alternative criterion for including an industry as low-wage its low-wage status in at least ten states.

5. U.S. Bureau of the Census, *Income of Families and Persons in the United States: 1963*, Current Population Reports, Series P–60, no. 43, (Washington: Government Printing Office, 1964), tables 11, 28.

6. Vera C. Perrella, "Low Earners and Their Incomes," *Monthly Labor Review*, May 1967, pp. 35–40. See also Laurie D. Cummings, "The Employed Poor: Their Characteristics and Occupations," *Monthly Labor Review*, July 1965, p. 830.

7. Steven Sternlieb and Alvin Bauman, "Employment Characteristics of Low-Wage Workers," *Monthly Labor Review*, July 1965, pp. 11–12.

8. Barry Bluestone, "Low Wage Industries and the Working Poor," *Poverty and Human Resources Abstracts*, March–April 1968, pp. 6–7.

9. SICs 253, 259 "Other Furniture and Fixtures," were not listed for 1958, but should have been, since their average hourly earnings were $1.85. The same is true of SIC 367, "Electronic Components and Accessories," and SIC 385, "Ophthalmic Goods."

10. Delehanty and Evans, "Low-Wage Employment," pp. 29, 76–80. Other listings of low-wage occupations based on the 1960 census include Cummings, "The Employed Poor," p. 832, 833 tables 4–5, who provides an actual count of individuals in selected low-wage occupations earning less than $3,000 in 1959, and Max A. Rutzick, "A Ranking of U.S. Occupations by Earnings," *Monthly Labor Review*, March 1965, pp. 249–255.

11. "Identification of the Poor," *Monthly Labor Review*, March 1965, pp. 306–307. Paul M. Ryscavage, "Economic Developments in Urban Poverty Neighborhoods," *Monthly Labor Review*, June 1969, pp. 51–56, contrasts the percentage distribution by broad occupational groups of the employed living in urban poverty neighborhoods and in other urban neighborhoods.

12. See John E. Buckley, "Wage Dispersion in Metropolitan Areas," *Monthly Labor Review*, September 1969, pp. 24–29.

13. Irving Morrisett, *The Economic Structure of American Cities*, The Regional Science Association, *Papers*, vol. 4, (Philadelphia, 1958), pp. 239–256.

14. U.S. Department of Commerce, Business and Defense Services Administration, *Metropolitan Area and City Size Patterns of Manufacturing Industries 1954*, Area Trend Series no. 4, (Washington: Government Printing Office, June 1959).

15. Victor R. Fuchs, *Differentials in Hourly Earnings by Region and City Size, 1959*, Occasional Paper 101, National Bureau of Economic Research, (New York, 1967).

16. H. M. Douty, "Wage Differentials: Forces and Counter Forces," *Monthly Labor Review*, March 1968, pp. 74–81.

17. Kenneth J. Hoffman, "Metropolitan Area Pay Levels and Trends," *Monthly Labor Review*, April 1968, pp. 44–49.

18. Donald J. Blackmore, "Occupational Wage Relationships in Metropolitan Areas," *Monthly Labor Review*, December 1968, pp. 29–36; especially Tables 1, 3.

19. Carl Rosenfeld and Kathryn Gover, "Employment of School-Age Youth," *Monthly Labor Review*, August 1972, p. 30.

20. Vera C. Perrella, "Young Workers and Their Earnings," *Monthly Labor Review*, July 1971, p. 4.

21. Vera C. Perrella, "Employment of High School Graduates and Dropouts in 1968," *Monthly Labor Review*, June 1969, p. 41.

22. Edward Kalachek, "Determinants of Teen-

age Employment," *Journal of Human Resources,* Winter 1969, p. 8.

23. Forrest Bogan, "Employment of School Age Youth," *Monthly Labor Review,* October 1968, chart.

24. Edward Kalachek, *The Youth Labor Market,* (Ann Arbor: Institute of Labor and Industrial Relations The University of Michigan—Wayne State University and the National Manpower Policy Task Force), p. 57.

25. Perrella, "Employment of High School Graduates," p. 40.

26. Perrella, "Low Earners and Their Incomes," pp. 35–37.

27. Bluestone, "Low Wage Industries," pp. 6–7.

28. Valerie K. Oppenheimer, "The Sex-Labelling of Jobs," *Industrial Relations,* May 1968, p. 220.

29. U.S. Equal Employment Opportunity Commission, *Job Patterns for Minorities and Women in Private Industry 1966,* (Equal Employment Opportunity Report no. 1), undated, pt. 1, pp. F–4, 5.

30. Oppenheimer, "Sex-Labelling of Jobs," p. 255. See also *Census of Population: 1960,* "Occupational Characteristics," Final Report PC (2)–7A, Tables 9 and 28.

31. Calvin F. Schmid, "Socioeconomic Differentials Among Non-White Races," *American Sociological Review,* December 1965, pp. 90–99. U.S. Bureau of the Census, *Census of Population: 1970* Final Reports PC(2)–1B, D, E and G.

32. U.S. Equal Employment Opportunity Commission, *Job Patterns*, pp. A1–4. (For information on nonwhites see Bureau of Labor Statistics, *The Negroes in the United States—Their Economic and Social Situation*, Bulletin no. 1511, (Washington: U.S. Government Printing Office, June 1966), pp. 114–121.

33. U.S. EEOC, *Job Patterns*, pp. B1–4.

34. Bureau of Labor Statistics, *Negroes in the U.S.*, pp. 15–16. For slightly greater occupational detail on nonwhite employment and trends from 1956–67, see Claire C. Hodge, "The Negro Job Situation: Has it Improved?," *Monthly Labor Review*, January 1969, pp. 20–28.

35. U.S. Equal Employment Opportunity Commission, *Job Patterns*, pt. 3, pp. 201–211. See also the report by the same title for 1970, vol. 2, pp. 449–462.

36. Ibid., pt. 1, p. 8.

37. Elizabeth Waldman, "Educational Attainment of Workers," *Monthly Labor Review*, February 1969, pp. 14–22. See also *Census of Population: 1960*, vol. 2, "Occupation by Earnings and Education," Final Report PC(2)–7B, Table 1.

38. Fuchs, *Differentials in Hourly Earnings*, pp. 27–32.

39. David P. Taylor, "Discrimination and Occupational Wage Differences in the Market for Unskilled Labor," *Industrial and Labor Relations Review*, April 1969, pp. 375–390.

40. U.S. Bureau of the Census, *Educational Attainment: March 1972*, Current Population Reports, Series P-20, no. 243 (Washington: Government Printing Office, 1972), pp. 14, 15.

41. Harvey R. Hamel, "Educational Attainment of Workers," *Monthly Labor Review*, February 1968, p. 33.

42. Charles C. Killingsworth, *Jobs and Incomes for Negroes*, The Institute of Labor and Industrial Relations and National Manpower Policy Task Force, May 1968, pp. 24–26.

43. Max A. Rutzick, "A Ranking of U.S. Occupations by Earnings," *Monthly Labor Review*, March 1965, pp. 249–255.

44. O. D. Duncan, "Occupational Components of Educational Differences in Income," *Journal of the American Statistical Association*, December 1961, pp. 783–792.

45. Delehanty and Evans, "Low-Wage Employment," pp. 37–40.

46. Denis F. Johnston, "Education and Training Requirements for Occupations in March 1965," *Monthly Labor Review*, March 1966, pp. 250–257.

47. Waldman, "Educational Attainment of Workers," p. 20.

48. Hamel, "Educational Attainment of Workers," pp. 29, 32; Denis F. Johnston, "Education and the Labor Force," *Monthly Labor Review*, September 1968, pp. 1–11.

49. Mary Jean Bowman, "Human Inequalities and Southern Economic Development," *The Southern Economic Journal Supplement*, July 1965, pp. 97–98.

50. Stephen Michelson, "Rational Income Decisions of Negroes and Everybody Else," *Industrial and Labor Relations Review*, October 1969, pp. 15–28; Gary S. Becker, *The Economics of*

Discrimination (Chicago: The University of Chicago Press, 1957), pp. 92–93.

51. Roy Lassiter, Jr., "The Association of Income and Education for Males by Region, Race, and Age," *Southern Economic Journal,* July 1965, pp. 15–22.

52. Estimated from U.S. Bureau of the Census, *Income in 1967 of Families in the United States,* Current Population Reports, Series P–60, no. 59, (Washington: Government Printing Office, April 18, 1969), p. 41. (For families with four or more workers it was assumed that there were three secondary workers.)

53. Ibid., p. 18.

54. Estimated from Elizabeth Waldman and Yvonne C. Olson, "Unemployment in the American Family," *Monthly Labor Review,* October 1968, p. 44 (Table 4).

55. Elizabeth Waldman, "Marital and Family Characteristics of Workers, March 1966," *Monthly Labor Review,* April 1967, p. 35 (Table 3).

56. See Doris K. Lewis, "Prevalence of Disabilities in the Workforce," *Monthly Labor Review,* September 1964, pp. 1003, 1006–1007.

57. Carl Rosenfeld and Elizabeth Waldman, "Work Limitation and Chronic Health Problems," *Monthly Labor Review,* January 1967, pp. 38–41. All figures cited are derived from the Public Health Service. Other figures are available from the Social Security Administration which are quantitatively different, although the same conclusions would follow. See Lawrence D. Haber, "Disability, Work, and Income Maintenance: Prevalence of Disability, 1966," *Social Security Bulletin,* May

1968, pp. 14–23; and Lawrence D. Haber, "Identifying the Disabled: Concepts and Methods in Measurement of Disability," *Social Security Bulletin*, December 1967, pp. 17–34.

58. U.S. Advisory Council on Health Insurance for the Disabled, *Health Insurance Disability Under Social Security*, 1969, appendix B, Table A.

59. Paul O. Flaim, "Persons Not in the Labor Force: Who They Are and Why They Don't Work," *Monthly Labor Review*, July 1969, pp. 3–13.

60. Bureau of Labor Statistics, *The Negroes in the United States–Their Economic and Social Situation*, Bulletin no. 1511, (Washington: U.S. Government Printing Office, June 1966), pp. 228–229.

Chapter Four

1. Phillips Cutright, "Negro Subordination and White Gains," *American Sociological Review*, February 1965, pp. 110–112.

2. U.S. Equal Employment Opportunity Commission, *Job Patterns*, pt. 1, p. 3. Earlier Becker had reached similar conclusions. See Becker, *Economics of Discrimination*, pp. 92–93, 105.

3. Becker, *Economics of Discrimination*, pp. 92–93, 105.

4. Hamel, "Educational Attainment of Workers," pp. 26–34, Table 3.

5. H. J. Gilman, "Economic Discrimination and Unemployment," *American Economic Review*, December 1965, pp. 1077–1096.

6. Victor Fuchs, "Differences in Hourly Earn-

ings between Men and Women," *Monthly Labor Review*, May 1971, pp. 9–15.

7. Henry Sanborn, "Pay Differences Between Men and Women," *Industrial and Labor Relations Review*, July 1964, pp. 534–550.

8. Donald J. McNulty, "Differences in Pay between Men and Women Workers," *Monthly Labor Review*, December 1967, pp. 4–43.

9. *Getting Hired, Getting Trained–A Study of Industry Practices and Policies on Youth Employment*, National Committee on Employment of Youth (New York, 1964), p. 26.

10. Daniel E. Diamond and Hrach Bedrosian, *Industry Hiring Requirements and the Employment of Disadvantaged Groups*, (New York: New York University School of Commerce, 1970). See also Gloria Shaw Hamilton and J. David Roessner, "How Employers Screen Disadvantaged Job Applicants," *Monthly Labor Review*, September 1972, pp. 14–21.

11. James G. Scoville, "Education and Training Requirements for Occupations," *Review of Economics and Statistics*, November 1966, pp. 387–394.

12. James R. Bright, "The Relationship of Increasing Automation and Skill Requirements," in Report of the National Commission on Technology, Automation, and Economic Progress, *Technology and the American Economy* (Washington: U.S. Government Printing Office, February 1966), Appendix, vol. 2, pp. 214, 220.

13. Scoville, "Education and Training Requirements," p. 391.

14. Robert L. Raimon and Vladimir Stoikov, "The Quality of the Labor Forces," *Industrial and Labor Relations Review*, April 1967, pp. 391–413.

15. Charles C. Killingsworth, "The Continuing Labor Market Twist," *Monthly Labor Review*, September 1968, pp. 12–17. See also Denis F. Johnston, "The Labor Market Twist, 1964–1969," *Monthly Labor Review*, July 1971, pp. 26–37, which finds that the trends noted by Killingsworth have slowed down.

16. Ronald E. Kutscher and Eva E. Jacobs, "Factors Affecting Changes in Industry Employment," *Monthly Labor Review*, April 1967, pp. 6–12.

17. Victor R. Fuchs, *The Service Economy* (New York: National Bureau of Economic Research, Columbia University Press, 1968), p. 84.

18. Ibid., pp. 42, 445. The term "income elasticity" refers to the percentage change in amount demanded divided by the percentage change in income with which it is associated.

19. Delehanty and Evans, "Low-Wage Employment," pp. 10–11.

20. Ibid., pp. 19–20.

21. Fuchs, *The Service Economy*, pp. 6–8, 136, 245–251.

22. Ibid., pp. 216–218; Delehanty and Evans, "Low-Wage Employment," p. 22.

23. Bert G. Hickman, *Investment Demand and U.S. Economic Growth* (Washington: The Brookings Institution, 1965), pp. 230–231.

24. Genevieve B. Wimsatt and John T. Woodward, "Revised Estimates of New Plant and

Equipment Expenditures in the United States, 1947–1969: Part I," *Survey of Current Business*, January 1970, pp. 25–39, Table 1.

25. Delehanty and Evans, "Low-Wage Employment," pp. 10–11.

26. Fuchs, *The Service Economy*, pp. 84, 96.

27. *Research and Development in Industry, 1970*, National Science Foundation, Surveys of Science Resources Series, NSF 72-309, p. 34.

28. Fuchs, *The Service Economy*, pp. 87–88; and Henry Linsert, Jr., "An Empirical Study of the Relationships Between Output per Manhour and Related Variables in Manufacturing Industries, 1954 to 1963." Master's thesis, George Washington University, 1970, p. 57.

29. This factor is stressed by Killingsworth with special regard to nonwhites in *Jobs and Incomes for Negroes*, pp. 7–10. See also John F. Cain and Joseph J. Persky, "The Nation's Stake in Southern Rural Poverty," Program on Regional and Urban Economics, Discussion Paper no. 18, Mimeographed. Cambridge, Mass.: Harvard, May 1967.

30. Alfred Tella, "Labor Force Sensitivity to Employment by Age and Sex," *Industrial Relations*, February 1965, pp. 69–83.

31. Vera C. Perrella, "Women and the Labor Force," *Monthly Labor Review*, February 1968, pp. 1–9.

32. *Manpower Report of the President, 1970*, A Report on Manpower Requirements, Resources, Utilization, and Training Prepared by the United States Department of Labor, Transmitted to the Congress March 1970, pp. 241, 260; and see

Elizabeth Waldman, "Changes in the Labor Force Activity of Women," *Monthly Labor Review*, June 1970, p. 14.

33. Edward J. O'Boyle, "Job Tenure: How It Relates to Race and Age," *Monthly Labor Review*, September 1969, pp. 16–23.

34. Rosenfeld and Perrella, "Why Women Start and Stop Working," pp. 1077–1080.

35. Alfred Tella, "Labor Force Sensitivity to Employment by Age and Sex," *Industrial Relations*, February 1965, pp. 69–83.

36. *Manpower Report of the President, 1973*, p. 128.

37. O'Boyle, "Job Tenure," Table 2.

38. See Curtis L. Smith, "The Unemployed: Why They Started Looking for Work," *Monthly Labor Review*, October 1965, pp. 1196–1203.

39. Kalachek, *Youth Labor Market*, pp. 23–25. See also Kalachek, "Determinants of Teenage Unemployment," pp. 17–18.

40. Yale Brozen, "The Effect of Statutory Minimum Wage Increases on Teenage Unemployment," *Journal of Law and Economics*, April 1969, pp. 109–122. See also Thomas G. Moore, "The Effect of Minimum Wages on Teenage Unemployment," *Journal of Political Economy*, July/August 1971, pp. 897–902.

41. *Manpower Report of the President, 1972*, pp. 165, 166.

42. Flaim, "Persons Not in the Labor Force," pp. 8, 11, 12, Tables 1–3, and Susan Holland, "Adult Men Not in the Labor Force," *Monthly Labor Review*, March 1967, pp. 5–15.

43. Robert L. Stein, "Reasons for Nonparticipation in the Labor Force," *Monthly Labor Review*, July 1967, pp. 22–27.

44. Harvey R. Hamel, "Moonlighting: An Economic Phenomenon," *Monthly Labor Review*, October 1967, pp. 17–22.

45. U.S., Congress, House, Special Subcommittee on Labor of the Committee on Education and Labor on H. R. 12667, *Employment of "Green Card" Aliens During Labor Disputes*, 91st Cong., 1st sess., 1969; United States Commission on Civil Rights, "The Commuter on the United States– Mexico Border," pp. 155–180. *Amendment of Immigration and Nationality Act*–Alien Commuter (Green Card) System, Congressional Record, 90th Cong., 1st Sess., 1967, pp. 36828–36833.

46. "Aliens in the Fields: The 'green card commuter' under the Immigration and Naturalization Laws," *Stanford Law Review*, June 1969, p. 1765. (Data from Department of Labor, *Occupational Wage Structure, Laredo, Texas*, June 1961.)

47. Anna-Stina Ericson, "Impact of Commuters Across the Mexican Border," *Monthly Labor Review*, August 1970, p. 19. See also, Selection Commission on Western Hemisphere Immigration, *Report*, January 1968, Research Supplement, p. 115.

48. U.S., Congress, House, Committee on the Judiciary, *Review of the Operation of the Immigration and Nationality Act of October 3, 1965* (Hearings before Subcommittee no. 1), 90th Cong., 2d sess., 22 May 1968, p. 105, Table 3.

49. Ibid., pp. 108–109, Table 5.

50. Lawrence Fuico, "How the Mechanization of Harvesting is Affecting Jobs," *Monthly Labor Review*, March 1969, p. 27. See also Howard N. Dellon, "Foreign Agricultural Workers and the Prevention of Adverse Effect," *Labor Law Journal*, vol. 17, December 1966, pp. 739–748.

51. William E. Martin, "Alien Workers in U.S. Agriculture: Impact on Production," *Journal of Farm Economics*, December 1966, p. 1138.

52. Belton M. Fleischer, "Some Economic Aspects of Puerto Rican Migration to the United States." Ph.D. dissertation, Stanford University, 1961.

53. Stanley L. Friedlander, *Labor Migration and Economic Growth: A Case Study of Puerto Rico* (Cambridge: M.I.T. Press, 1965).

54. It should be added, however, that Puerto Ricans have been accustomed for a very long time to unemployment rates always well above 10 percent; that their labor force participation rates in the prime working age groups for males tend to be well below U.S. levels; and that the greater persistence of an extended family system in the Puerto Rican community, with the extended family reaching across the sea from Puerto Rico to New York, means that the higher unemployment rate means little as long as it is accompanied by high employment at wages far above those previously earned in Puerto Rico. Thus, high unemployment rates for Puerto Ricans in New York may overstate the adverse impacts of migration and the extent to which it resulted in unemployment. Evidence of adjustments in the past in migration flows respon-

sive to changing economic conditions in New York, and also to changing conditions in Puerto Rico more recently, suggests that it is not really a disequilibrium situation, far though it is from an optimum.

55. Department of Labor, Manpower Administration, *Area Trends in Employment and Unemployment,* issues from September 1962 to September 1963.

56. U.S. Equal Employment Opportunities Commission, *Job Patterns,* pt. 3, pp. 201–211.

57. See Killingsworth, *Jobs and Income for Negroes,* p. 44, and Edward C. Banfield, *The Unheavenly City* (Boston: Little, Brown & Co., 1970), pp. 100–106, 112.

58. Richard Bloom, Martin Whiteman, and Martin Deutsch, "Race and Social Class as Separate Factors Related to Social Environment," *American Journal of Sociology,* January 1965, pp. 471–476.

59. Leonard Goodwin, *Do the Poor Want to Work: Studies in the Work Orientation of the Poor and the Non-Poor,* (Washington, D.C.: The Brookings Institution, 1972).

60. Paul Delaney, "Bitterness, Confusion Mark New Workfare Program," *Evening Star and Daily News,* (Washington, D.C.), 10 October 1972.

61. Joan S. Lublin, "Forced Labor? " *Wall Street Journal,* 20 October 1972.

62. The term, as well as the concept, of a way of life among the poor transcending national and ethnic lines probably originated with Oscar Lewis. See his *The Children of Sanchez,* (New York:

Random House, Vintage Books, 1961), pp. xxiv–xxvii.

63. Banfield, *Unheavenly City*, chapters 3, 10, pp. 125–131.

64. Michael J. Piore, *Public and Private Responsibilities in On-the-Job Training of Disadvantaged Workers*, M.I.T. Department of Economics, Working Paper no. 23 (Cambridge, Mass., June 1968).

65. For views sharply at variance with Banfield's, see Kenneth B. Clark, "Education of the Minority Poor—The Key to the War on Poverty," in *The Disadvantaged Poor: Education and Employment* (Washington: Chamber of Commerce of the United States, 1966), pp. 173–188.

66. Myron L. Joseph, "Job Vacancy Measurement," *Journal of Human Resources*, Fall 1966, pp. 59–80.

67. Raymond A. Konstant and Irwin O. Winegard, "Analysis and Use of Job Vacancy Statistics: Part I," *Monthly Labor Review*, August 1968, pp. 22–31.

68. Ibid., pt. 2, September 1968, pp. 18–22.

69. John G. Myers, "Conceptual and Measurement Problems in Job Vacancies: A Progress Report on the NICB Study," *The Measurement and Interpretation of Job Vacancies* (New York: Columbia University Press, 1966), p. 421.

70. Lloyd Ulman, "Labor Mobility and the Industrial Wage Structure in the Postwar U.S.," *Quarterly Journal of Economics*, April 1968, pp. 73–97.

71. Paul M. Ryscavage and Hazel M. Willacy,

"Employment of the Nation's Poor," *Monthly Labor Review*, August 1968, p. 18.

72. Thomas Dernberg and Kenneth Strand, "Hidden Unemployment 1953–62: A Quantitative Analysis by Age and Sex," *American Economic Review*, March 1966, pp. 71–95.

73. Joseph D. Mooney, "Urban Poverty and Labor Force Participation," *American Economic Review*, March 1967, pp. 104–199.

74. Larry D. Singel, "Some Private and Social Aspects of the Labor Mobility of Young Workers," *Quarterly Review of Economics and Business*, Spring 1966, pp. 19–28.

75. Melvin Lurie, "Racial Differences in Migration and Job Search: A Case Study," *Southern Economic Journal*, July 1966, pp. 81–95.

76. Graham L. Reid, "Job Search and Effectiveness of Job-Finding Methods," *Industrial and Labor Relations Review*, July 1972, pp. 479–495.

77. Myers, "Conceptual and Measurement Problems," pp. 405–437.

78. John G. Myers, *Job Vacancies in the Firm and Labor Market*, National Industrial-Conference Board Studies in Business Economics no. 109, (New York, 1969), pp. 80–96.

79. Samuel Saben, "Geographic Mobility and Employment Status, March 1962–March 1963," *Monthly Labor Review*, August 1964, pp. 873–881.

80. Dale E. Hathaway and Brian B. Perkins, "Farm Labor, Mobility, and Income Distribution," *American Journal of Agricultural Economics*, May 1968, pp. 342–353.

81. David Rasmussen, "The Effect of Regional

and Occupational Mobility on Non-White Income Changes, 1950–1960," Washington University Institute for Urban and Regional Studies Working Paper EDA 6, (St. Louis, January 1968).

82. U.S. Bureau of the Census, Census of Population 1970, *Mobility for States and the Nation*, PC(2)–2B (Washington: Government Printing Office, 1973), Tables 5, 6, 20. See also Charles F. Haywood, "The Unemployed Poor: Labor Mobility and Poverty," in *The Disadvantaged Poor: Education and Employment* (Washington: Chamber of Commerce of the United States, 1966), pp. 265–295.

83. Audrey Freedman, "Labor Mobility Projects for the Unemployed," *Monthly Labor Review*, June 1968, pp. 56–62.

84. Warren F. Mazek, "Unemployment and the Efficacy of Migration: The Case of Laborers," *Journal of Regional Science*, April 1969, pp. 101–107.

85. Saben, "Geographic Mobility," pp. 873–881.

86. Peter M. Blau, "The Flow of Occupational Supply and Recruitment," *American Sociological Review*, August 1965, pp. 475–490.

87. Bruce K. Eckland, "Academic Mobility, Higher Education, and Occupational Mobility," *American Sociological Review*, October 1965, pp. 735–746.

88. Richard A. Rehberg and David L. Westby, "Parental Encouragement, Occupation, Education, and Family Sizes: Artifactual or Independent Determinants of Adolescent Educational Expecta-

tions?," *Social Forces*, March 1967, pp. 362–374. See also William H. Sewell, Archibald D. Haller and Alejandro Portes, "The Educational and Early Occupational Attainment Process," *American Sociological Review*, February 1969, pp. 82–92.

89. Lamar B. Jones and James W. Christian, "Some Observations on the Agricultural Labor Market," *Industrial and Labor Relations Review*, July 1965, pp. 524–526.

90. Dale E. Hathaway, "Occupational Mobility from the Farm Labor Force," in C. E. Bishop, ed., *Farm Labor in the United States* (New York: Columbia University Press, 1967), p. 90.

91. Hirschel Kasper, "The Asking Price of Labor and the Duration of Unemployment," *Review of Economics and Statistics*, May 1967, pp. 165–172.

92. Paul Kear, "Long Run Changes in Occupational Wage Structure, 1900–1956," *Journal of Political Economy*, December 1960, pp. 584–600. See also Harry Ober, "Occupational Wage Differentials: 1907–1947," *Monthly Labor Review*, July 1948, pp. 127–134.

93. Martin Segal, "Occupational Wage Differentials in Major Cities During the 1950's," *Human Resources in the Urban Economy* (Baltimore: The Johns Hopkins Press, Resources for the Future, 1963), pp. 195–207.

94. Malcolm S. Cohen, "The Effect of Wages on the Relative Employment of Unskilled Labor," *Technology and the American Economy* (Washington, D.C.: U.S. Government Printing Office), Appendix, vol. 3, pp. 247–267.

95. Delehanty and Evans, "Low-Wage Employment," p. 54.

96. Stuart O. Schweitzer, "Factors Determining the Interindustry Structure of Wages," *Industrial and Labor Relations Review*, January 1969, pp. 217–225.

Chapter Five

1. John M. Peterson and Charles T. Stewart, Jr., *Employment Effects of Minimum Wages* (Washington: American Enterprise Institute for Public Policy Research, 1969), p. 19.

2. Fuchs, *The Service Economy*, p. 96. Elastic demand in this context means that demand increases more than in proportion to increases in income.

3. For a summary of a number of studies, see Werner Z. Hirsch, *The Economics of State and Local Government* (New York: McGraw-Hill, 1970), pp. 130–132. An elastic price response means that the percentage change in amount demanded is greater than the percentage change in price.

4. John F. Due, "Studies of State–Local Tax Influences on Location of Industry," *National Tax Journal*, June 1961, pp. 163–173.

5. For a recent assessment of these diverse effects, see Bureau of Labor Statistics, *Youth Unemployment and Minimum Wages*, Bulletin 1657, (Washington: Government Printing Office, 1970).

6. Reynolds Nowell, "A Plan for Youth Em-

ployment," in *The Disadvantaged Poor: Education and Employment* (Washington: Chamber of Commerce of the United States, 1966), pp. 323–343.

7. Lester Thurow, "Tax Credits for Training the Disadvantaged." Mimeographed. Washington, D.C.: Urban Coalition and The Brookings Institution, March 1969.

8. Sar Levitan, Garth Mangum, and Robert Taggart III, *Economic Opportunity in the Ghetto: The Partnership of Government and Business* (Baltimore: The Johns Hopkins University Press, 1970), pp. 30–32.

9. James M. Buchanan and John E. Moes, "A Regional Countermeasure to National Wage Standardization," *American Economic Review*, June 1960, pp. 434–438.

10. See John E. Moes, "The Subsidization of Industry by Local Communities in the South," *Southern Economic Journal*, October 1961, pp. 187–193. See also the comments by Irving Goffman and James Thompson in the October 1962 issue, pp. 111–119.

11. Garth L. Mangum, "Guaranteeing Employment Opportunities," *Social Policies for America in the Seventies: Nine Divergent Views* (Garden City, N. J.: Doubleday & Company, 1968), pp. 25–55.

12. Sar A. Levitan and Garth L. Mangum, *Federal Training and Work Programs in the Sixties* (Ann Arbor: Institute of Labor and Industrial Relations, 1969), pts. 4–6; Sar A. Levitan, Martin Rein, and David Marwick, *Work and Welfare Go Together* (Baltimore: The Johns Hopkins University Press, 1972), chapters 4, 5.

13. See National Industrial Conference Board, *Education, Training and Employment of the Disadvantaged*, Public Affairs Study no. 4, (New York, 1969), pp. 28–29, 45–46; and Louis A. Ferman, *Job Development for the Hard to Employ* (Ann Arbor: University of Michigan, Wayne State University Institute of Labor and Industrial Relations, and West Virginia University Center for Appalachian Studies and Development, 1969), pp. 4–36.

14. See Ferman, *Job Development*, p. 4–36.

15. National Industrial Conference Board, *Education, Training and Employment*, pp. 44–45.

16. Ibid., pp. 2–4.

17. Levitan and Mangum, *Federal Training*, pt. 7.

18. Gordon C. Cameron, *Regional Economic Development—The Federal Role* (Baltimore: The Johns Hopkins Press, Resources for the Future, 1970).

19. Linsert, Output per Manhour, p. 58.

20. Fuchs, *The Service Economy*, pp. 90–91.

21. Department of Labor, Women's Bureau, *British Policies and Methods in Employing Women in Wartime*, Bulletin no. 200, 1944, page 14.

22. Larry A. Sjaastad, "The Costs and Returns of Human Migration," *Journal of Political Economy*, October 1962, *Supplement*, pp. 80–93.

23. Audrey Freedman, "Labor Mobility Projects for the Unemployed," *Monthly Labor Review*, June 1968, pp. 56–62.

24. Arnold L. Nemore and Garth L. Mangum, *Reorienting the Federal–State Employment Service* (Ann Arbor: Institute of Labor and Industrial

Relations, The University of Michigan and Wayne State University, and the National Manpower Policy Task Force, 1968).

25. Banfield takes an extreme position, arguing that many children who are not college bound will benefit little from academic education after age fourteen, and many will be harmed by it. He recommends work starting at fourteen instead of academic high school graduation. (See Banfield, *Unheavenly City*, pp. 132–157.) The prospect of lowering the compulsory maximum age of school attendance seems as quixotic as his proposal to lower the minimum working age to fourteen.

26. *Manpower Report of the President 1970*, pp. 258, 226, 302.

27. George E. Johnson, "The Demand for Labor by Educational Category," *Southern Economic Journal*, October 1970, pp. 190–204. Additional education therefore does not offer the prospect of greatly reducing the share of low-productivity occupations in the labor market. It will, of course, improve the training and employment options of many individuals. Those with relatively less education may remain at a relative disadvantage, whatever the absolute level of attainment.

28. Vera C. Perrella and Edward J. O'Boyle, "Work Plans of Men Not in the Labor Force," *Monthly Labor Review*, August 1968, pp. 8–13.

29. Gerald G. Somers and W. D. Wood, eds., *Cost Benefit Analysis of Manpower Policies* (Proceedings of a North American Conference, sponsored by Center for Studies in Vocational and

Technical Education, University of Wisconsin, and the Industrial Relations Center, Queens University, Kingston: Hanson and Edgar, Ltd., 1970); Gerald G. Somers, ed., *Retraining the Unemployed* (Madison: University of Wisconsin Press, 1968).

30. Garth L. Mangum, *Reorienting Vocational Education* (Ann Arbor: Institute of Labor Relations, University of Michigan, Wayne State University, and National Manpower Policy Task Force, 1968). Jacob J. Kaufman et al., An Analysis of Comparative Costs and Benefits of Vocational vs. Academic Education in Secondary Schools. Mimeographed. University Park, Penn.: Institute for Research on Human Resources, Pennsylvania State University, October, 1967.

31. Leonard J. Hausman, "The Welfare Tax Rate: Its Relationship to the Employability and 'Self-Supportability' of AFDC Recipients." Paper presented at the Conference of New Manpower Researchers in Washington D.C., sponsored by the Department of Labor, 1967. Mimeographed.

32. Levitan, Rein, and Marwick, *Work and Welfare*, pp. 79–82, 102–105.

Index

Agriculture: demand elasticity in, 77; low wages of, 17; migration from, 111; productivity trends in, 77; research about, 81

Aid to Families with Dependent Children (AFDC), 191–92

Alien international commuters, 91–92

Alien farm workers: decline in, 94; numbers of, 93; regional concentration of, 95

Aliens. *See* Immigrant workers

American Indians, occupation of, 41–42

Apparel industry: earnings of, 79; employment trends in, 77; low wages of, 17; protection of, 77; and Puerto Rican migration to New York, 95; research about, 81

Banfield, Edward C., 99, 238 n

Bauman, Alvin, 19

Becker, Gary S., 64

Bedrosian, Hrach, 68

Blackmore, Donald J., 33, 40

Blau, Peter M., 114

Bluestone, Barry, 20

Bright, James R., 71–72

Brozen, Yale, 89

Buchanan, James M., 150–51

Chinese, occupation of, 41–42

Clague, Ewan, 72

Cohen, Malcolm S., 117

Cubans in Miami: occupation of, 96–97; unemployment of, 96

Delehanty, George E., 15–17, 20–22, 26, 28

Demand for low-skill workers: adjustment in, 7, 8; policy to increase, 144; and technological trends, 71–72, 74; and trends for low-skill occupations, 71, 72; and trends for low-wage industry, 73; and

241